GLOBAL JUSTICE NOW!

IMF/WORLD BANK
50 YEARS IS ENOUGH

WTO · IMF · WORLD BANK

EMPTY PROMISES
*The IMF, the World Bank,
and the Planned Failures of Global Capitalism*

*Thanks to ALL who
helped make this booklet
and our work possible.*

S0-AGC-510

**50 Years Is Enough:
U.S. Network
for Global
Economic Justice**
is a coalition of over 200
U.S. grassroots, women's,
solidarity, faith-based, policy,
social- and economic- justice,
youth, labor and
development organizations
dedicated to the profound
transformation of the World
Bank and the IMF. We were
founded in 1994, on the
occasion of the 50th
anniversary of the creation of
the institutions. The
Network works in solidarity
with over 185 international
partner organizations in more
than 65 countries. Through
education and action, the
Network is committed to
ending the external
imposition of neo-liberal
economic programs, and to
making the development
process democratic and
accountable. We focus on
action-oriented economic
literacy, public mobilization,
and policy advocacy.

TABLE OF CONTENTS

Preface   **4**

Demands of the IMF & World Bank
50 Years Is Enough Network   **9**

Basic Facts About the IMF & World Bank
50 Years Is Enough Network   **13**

Debt - The Linchpin of Structural Adjustment & Globalization
Jubilee USA Network   **16**

Structural Adjustment
Maryknoll Office for Global Concerns   **18**

What's In A Name?: PRSP and Structural Adjustment
Focus on the Global South   **20**

The Failures of IMF/World Bank "Debt Relief"
Social Justice Committee   **22**

False Start: The IMF's Sovereign Debt Restructuring Mechanism
Halifax Initiative   **23**

The World Bank's International Development Association:
Developing Whom?
Halifax Initiative   **26**

The International Finance Corporation
50 Years Is Enough Network   **27**

MIGA: Taxpayer-Funded Profit Insurance from the World Bank
50 Years Is Enough Network   **29**

Impact of IMF and World Bank Policies on Labor
Global Unions (ICFTU)   **31**

Globalization and Women
Sisters of the Holy Cross   **33**

The World Bank and Health
50 Years Is Enough Network   **35**

HIV/AIDS: World's Worst Epidemic, Fuelled by Debt
& IMF/World Bank Policies
Africa Action   **37**

Pulling the TRIPS-Wire: Intellectual Property Rights & Public Health
Essential Action   **40**

Education: A Public Right or a Private Commodity?
50 Years Is Enough Network   **42**

The Drive for Water Privatization
Anti-Privatisation Forum   **44**

Land Reform
Food First   **46**

The Private Sector Development Strategy of the World Bank Group
Citizens Network on Essential Services   **48**

FTAA, CAFTA, PPP, IIRSA: Latin America's Alphabet Soup of Neo-liberalism
ACERCA / Action for Social and Ecological Justice (ASEJ)   **50**

GATS: In Whose Service?
Alliance for Democracy   **52**

The World Bank and Free Trade: Working in Harmony
Jubilee USA Network / RESULTS   **54**

The World Bank and Large Dams
International Rivers Network   **56**

The World Bank's Corporate Agenda: Enron and Oil for the Global North
Sustainable Energy & Economy Network (SEEN) / Institute for Policy Studies   **58**

Export Credit Agencies: The Dirtiest Secret of Globalization
Pacific Environment   **60**

Microcredit: Can it Survive the World Bank's Help?
50 Years Is Enough Network   **62**

Post-Conflict Countries: East Timor
East Timor Action Network   **64**

Post-Conflict Countries: Sri Lanka
Movement for National Land and Agricultural Reform (MONLAR)   **66**

Argentina, the IMF, and the World Bank
Global Economy Project / Institute for Policy Studies   **68**

Human Rights, Oil, & Indigenous Communities:
The World Bank in the Andean Region
Center for Economic and Social Rights   **69**

Domestic Servitude & IMF/World Bank Staff
Break The Chain Campaign / Institute for Policy Studies   **72**

Act Locally for Global Justice: Join the World Bank Bonds Boycott
Center for Economic Justice / World Bank Bonds Boycott   **73**

List of Abbreviations   **75**

Resource Guide   **76**

EMPTY PROMISES
The IMF, the World Bank, and the Planned Failures of Global Capitalism

This booklet is an introduction to the institutional power structures that create and manage the contemporary global economy. The 50 Years Is Enough Network has, for the last ten years, focused on the roles of the International Monetary Fund (IMF) and the World Bank. As a consequence, *Empty Promises* focuses more on those institutions than it does on other major players, such as the World Trade Organization, the U.S. Treasury Department, or multinational corporations, though we by no means ignore them. In this booklet, you will find brief essays about most of the vital issues on which the IMF and World Bank have an impact.

We start, as our title indicates, from the conviction that the global economic and political system is imbalanced and unjust, and unlikely to become fair or sustainable without a fundamental shift — in assumptions, in values, and in attitudes about power. Until that happens, people will continue to suffer and die needlessly, the distribution of resources and opportunities will continue to be scandalously skewed, and the abuse of the enormous powers accumulated by a relative few will continue to grow.

We cannot claim to know precisely how to reverse the course the global economy has been set on. We believe that the movement for global justice, of which the 50 Years Is Enough Network has been an important part since its founding in 1994, has succeeded in educating many people around the world about the immoral inequalities of the current system. The analysis and education work of global justice campaigners has penetrated the myths of inevitability and impermeability (and for some, infallibility) that for decades enveloped the institutions of global finance. But the task of replacing today's global economic system with one that is both just and sustainable remains daunting. *Empty Promises* is one part of our effort to build a constituency for change through education and by exposing the failures of the system.

> *The global economic and political system is imbalanced and unjust, and unlikely to become fair or sustainable without a fundamental shift — in assumptions, in values, and in attitudes about power.*

We are working for change that will dislodge the economic organizing principle of the current system, profit, and replace it with a system based on justice and sustainability.

The leading international financial institutions (IFIs), the IMF and the World Bank, were founded in 1944 to guard against the

return of worldwide economic depression such as that of the 1930s. The IMF was originally assigned to monitor currency values and help avert balance-of-trade crises, and the World Bank was meant to make loans to re-develop war-torn countries. Over the years, those roles have changed and expanded. Beginning around 1980, the IFIs became much more powerful, as they began to design and impose economic policy programs for dozens of countries. It was about that time that Margaret Thatcher was elected in the U.K. and Ronald Reagan in the U.S., and the neo-liberal economic doctrine became entrenched at the IFIs. It was also, unfortunately, the moment when the international debt crises — spurred by years of extravagant lending and borrowing (much of it from the World Bank), the oil crisis, and the dramatic increase in U.S. interest rates — struck Latin America and, in short order, much of the Caribbean, Africa, and Asia. Those crises gave the IMF — at the time an under-utilized bureaucracy — the opening to step in and begin making emergency loans tied to economic policy conditions. Before long the World Bank, which continued to make loans for large infrastructure projects (themselves often disastrous), joined in by offering follow-up programs that reinforced IMF conditions.

Those conditions, called structural adjustment programs (SAPs), differed very little from country to country, and had by 1990 been imposed on the great majority of governments in the Global South (Africa, Asia-Pacific, Latin America and the Caribbean). SAPs, which were ostensibly designed to restore stressed economies to health and provide for the orderly repayment of debt, have failed spectacularly in their stated aims. Debt levels have tripled or quadrupled for many of the borrowing countries, the gap between rich and poor has grown dramatically, environments have been devastated, and in much of sub-Saharan Africa, the region receiving the greatest part of the institutions' attention, the standard of living and life expectancy have dropped.

But even after over 20 years of apparent failure, including the onset of "IMF riots" around the world, the IFIs keep requiring adoption of the same austerity policies. Such long-term failure affecting so many people and involving so much money should make us suspicious. Is it possible that the institutions are not failing at all — that they are doing precisely what they are meant to do?

We think so. The IMF and World Bank are controlled by their wealthiest contributors, the Group of Seven (G7) countries. The policies the institutions have imposed over the last 25 years have opened up economies around the world to multinational corporations and banks based in the G7 countries, allowing them much greater latitude to reap profits from high interest rates, exploit low-wage workers, extract natural resources, sell in local markets and vanquish local competitors, maintain a flow of low-cost commodities, and buy up publicly-owned companies and financial institutions. This is the core of corporate globalization, and the IFIs have been the key to instituting it as the global economic system. The fact that only a small percentage of the population in Southern countries benefits from these developments, and that most are thrown into higher-stress lives and often deeper poverty, is also part of corporate globalization.

Is it possible that the World Bank and IMF are not failing at all — that they are doing precisely what they are meant to do?

As this model of corporate globalization has become entrenched, the IMF and World Bank have claimed that their mission is to reduce poverty, make debt more manageable, and provide more opportunities and services for people in borrowing countries. We believe that this is the sincere intent for at least some of the staff at the IFIs. But the way in which the institutions are structured, and in particular the implicit imperative that their policies must benefit the powerful Northern elites, or at least not harm them, undermine both the accomplishment of that aim and, as time passes and evidence accumulates, the credibility of those who continue to claim it. The claimed missions of the IMF and World Bank are genuinely *empty promises*. The seeming failures of their policies have always been predictable; how, after all, could reducing a country's productive capacity, slashing services, and turning over ownership of national assets to foreign interests ever be viewed as a positive strategy? But those failures in the countries that borrow from the IMF and World Bank, planned as they must surely be, are, it turns out, essential to the operation of the highly exploitative form of capitalism we have today, in which the powerful actors can no longer be contained in national contexts, but seek their own growth and profits everywhere. The logic of this capitalism dictates that cheap materials and labor be always available, and that logic can only be overturned by a concerted transformation of the principles of the global economy.

The model created and spread by the IFIs has begun to be replicated in the U.S. and other rich countries, as even nominally "left" parties adopt the tenets of neo-liberal hyper-capitalism: reductions in government services, emphasis on competition and profit-making, greater flexibility and fewer responsibilities for businesses and owners of capital. A divided world is emerging — divided less along North/South lines as between owners of capital and servants of capital.

In many ways we are returning to conditions similar to those prevailing in 1900. In the Global South, the economic system closely resembles the days of imperial colonialism, with minimal political sovereignty and economics reduced to the question of what one can offer to "world markets" — meaning Europe, North America, and now Japan. In the Global North, de-regulation has granted corporations flexibility and profit opportunities they have not seen in a hundred years, and the gap between rich and poor is growing rapidly. The colonial era in the North was marked by massive inequality too, though then, as now, even the less-privileged in the North benefited materially from global economic relations.

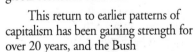

This return to earlier patterns of capitalism has been gaining strength for over 20 years, and the Bush Administration is pushing the agenda more rapidly than any U.S. administration before it. One function of the multilateral institutions has been to obscure the lines of responsibility and accountability, and periodic re-configurations are useful for preserving that accomplishment. In the current system, the IFIs can always, with some justification, say that they are just the servants of the G7 governments that control them (with the U.S. by far the first among equals). A change of course would require a change of will among the wealthy governments. Meanwhile, the G7 governments can say, also with some justification, that the policies causing such harm are made by technicians at the IFIs. The separation of political and technical responsibility has helped prevent opponents of these policies from effectively targeting a consistent enemy. And while this goes on, the rich keep getting richer.

As we seek fundamental change in the system explained in *Empty Promises*, we recognize the tremendous power of the system we must subvert. We maintain our hope by looking to the responses of people, everywhere in the world, when they learn how the system works. Outrage and determination to make a change are growing. And we know that the values of sustainability, of life over profit, are widely shared, are in fact the core of the belief systems even the most successful capitalists claim. And finally, we know that people are becoming more conscious of the failings in their various political systems, and of the prevalence of "interests" exercising control over political choices even in the most vaunted democracies. We have seen the determination of thousands of people to re-claim their politics and to insist that popular values become the genuine values of public institutions.

Even as we seek to understand its contemporary form, we must acknowledge that global capitalism is not a new phenomenon. It can be argued that it reached its most vile peak several centuries ago during the height of the slave trade, the most obscene extension of the logic of "free trade." Economic exploitation of resources and peoples in different parts of the world has continued since those days, and in the last 60 years has taken on a peculiarly bureaucratic face: oppression by treaty. But even in this guise, it has meant a slow-motion genocide and ecocide, playing out with hardly any notice, with plausible deniability for all its beneficiaries and agents. Our task is to stand in solidarity with those who live and often die from the effects and impacts of the system. Our task is to wake ourselves up, wake our fellow citizens up, and create a global system based on justice and sustainability, ecologically and economically. Otherwise, we will someday soon wake up to a world that can no longer bear its own weight. ∎

FOR FURTHER INFORMATION:

www.50years.org

50 Years Is Enough: U.S. Network for Global Economic Justice • Washington, DC USA

These demands were formulated by the 50 Years Is Enough Network through consultations over 15 months with the members of its South Council (representing social and economic justice organizations in 13 countries in Asia, Africa, Latin America, and the Caribbean) and others.

We call for the immediate suspension of the policies and practices of the International Monetary Fund (IMF) and World Bank Group which have caused widespread poverty, inequality, and suffering among the world's peoples and damage to the world's environment. Substantial responsibility for the unjust world economic system lies with those institutions and the World Trade Organization (WTO). We note that these institutions are anti-democratic, controlled by the G-7 governments, and that their policies have benefited international private sector financiers, transnational corporations, and corrupt officials and politicians.

We further call for the creation of a neutral and credible "Truth Commission," composed of individuals with a demonstrated commitment to poverty eradication and the health of the world's ecosystems, to investigate the actions and impacts of the IMF and the World Bank. The Truth Commission's findings must be respected and acted on by the governments, institutional officials, and civil society organizations concerned with economic development and international financial policies.

We issue this call in the name of global justice, in solidarity with the peoples of the Global South and the former "Soviet bloc" countries of Eastern Europe and Central Asia who struggle for survival and dignity in the face of unjust, imperialistic economic policies. We stand in solidarity too with the millions in the countries of the Global North who have borne the burden of "globalization" policies that mirror those imposed on the Global South.

Only when the coercive powers of the international financial institutions are eliminated shall governments be accountable first and foremost to the will of their peoples. Only when a system that allocates power chiefly to the wealthiest nations for the purpose of dictating policies to the weaker and impoverished ones is reversed shall peoples be able to forge bonds — economic and otherwise — based on mutual respect and the common needs of the planet and its inhabitants. Only when integrity is restored to economic development, and both the corrupter and the corrupted held accountable, shall the people begin to have confidence in the decisions that have impacts on their livelihoods and their communities. Only when the well-being of all, including the most vulnerable peoples and ecosystems, is given priority over corporate profits can we achieve genuine sustainable development and create a world of justice, equality, peace, and ecological values, where fundamental human rights, including internationally-recognized social, cultural, environmental, and economic rights, are respected.

With these ends in mind, we make the following demands of the management, executive directors, and Governors of the World Bank and the International Monetary Fund:

1. DEBT CANCELLATION: We demand that the IMF and World Bank cancel 100% of all claimed debts without imposing any form of external conditionalities. We concur with the position of Jubilee South that holds these debts to be illegitimate. Any funds required for this purpose should come from positive net capital and assets held by those institutions. Should other institutions, such as the African Development Bank, require assistance to write off the debts owed them, we call on the World Bank and IMF to make such funds available. We believe that civil society in the indebted countries should take the lead in determining how savings realized through cancellation are utilized.

2. END STRUCTURAL ADJUSTMENT: We demand that the IMF and World Bank immediately cease imposing the economic austerity measures known as structural adjustment and/or any other macroeconomic "reform" as conditions of loans, credits, or debt relief. This requires both the suspension of those conditions in existing programs and an abandonment of "poverty reduction strategy papers" (PRSPs) and any version of the Heavily Indebted Poor Countries (HIPC) Initiative, which conditions debt relief on policy reforms.

3. TRANSPARENCY: We demand that the IMF and World Bank Group make all board meetings public and all documents in its possession freely available to the public (with exceptions to protect confidentiality to be decided on by a neutral body). This includes all project and program agreements, board meeting minutes, evaluations of program failures and successes, etc. All documents must be made available in the local languages of project- and policy- affected peoples.

4. REPARATIONS FOR STRUCTURAL ADJUSTMENT:
We demand that the IMF and World Bank accept responsibility for
the disastrous impact of structural adjustment policies, as determined
by a neutral and credible Truth Commission, by paying reparations to
the peoples and communities who have borne the consequences.
These funds should come from the institutions' positive net capital
and assets, and should be distributed through democratically-
determined mechanisms.

**5. REPARATIONS FOR SOCIAL AND ECOLOGICAL
DEVASTATION:** We demand that the World Bank Group pay
reparations to peoples relocated and otherwise harmed by its large
projects (such as dams) and compensate governments for loan
repayments made on projects which World Bank evaluations rank as
economic failures. A further evaluation by a neutral and credible
Truth Commission should determine which World Bank projects
have failed on economic, social, cultural, and environmental grounds,
and see that appropriate compensation is made. The funds for these
payments should come from the institutions' positive net capital and
assets, and should be distributed through democratically-determined
mechanisms.

6. STOP AID TO PRIVATE SECTOR: (a) We demand that the
World Bank Group immediately cease providing advice and resources
to advance the goals associated with corporate globalization, such as
privatization and liberalization; (b) We demand that the International
Finance Corporation (IFC) and the Multilateral Investment Guaranty
Agency (MIGA) be closed, and that private-sector investments
currently held by these World Bank agencies be liquidated to provide
funds for the reparations demanded above.

7. ACCOUNTABILITY FOR CORRUPTION: We demand
that the agencies and individuals within the World Bank Group and
IMF complicit in abetting corruption, as well as their accomplices in
borrowing countries and in private banks, be prosecuted, with full
cooperation from the institutions, and that those responsible,
including the institutions, recover and return stolen wealth and
provide compensation for unrecoverable stolen resources. We call for
a neutral and credible Truth Commission to assess the culpability of
the various parties to corruption and stolen wealth.

8. ASSESSMENT OF INSTITUTIONS' FUTURE:

We demand that the future existence, structure, and policies of multilateral institutions such as the World Bank Group and the IMF be submitted to a re-evaluation conducted through a democratic, participatory and transparent process, building on the findings of a neutral and credible Truth Commission. The process must accord full participation to the peoples most affected by the policies and practices of the institutions, and include a significant and influential role for all parts of civil society, including farmers' associations, trade unions, women's organizations, non-governmental organizations, faith-based groups, and student/youth organizations.

The accession to these demands would require the institutions' directors to accept and act on the need for fundamental transformation. It is possible that the elimination of these institutions will be required for the realization of global economic and political justice.

We commit to work towards the defunding of the IMF and World Bank by opposing further government allocations to them (in the form of either direct contributions or the designation of collateral) and supporting campaigns such as a boycott of World Bank bonds until these demands have been met. ∎

50 Years Is Enough Network
3628 12th Street, NE
Washington, DC 20017
TEL +1-202-IMF-BANK
FAX +1-202-636-4238
EMAIL info@50years.org
WEB www.50years.org

History

The IMF and World Bank were founded in 1944 at a conference sponsored by the U.S. and U.K. governments in Bretton Woods, New Hampshire. As World War II was winding down, the Allies were beginning to consider how the new global economy should be ordered. Their primary goal was to avert the sort of financial imbalances that led to the Great Depression of the 1930s, and contributed to the rise of totalitarian demagogues in Europe. The IMF was considered the base institution — a monitor of national economies which oversaw currency values, and a kind of credit union to which national governments contributed money and from which they could take short-term loans in the event of balance-of-payment difficulties. The International Bank for Reconstruction and Development (IBRD), which would later evolve into the World Bank Group, was designed to make loans for rebuilding war-torn countries and developing non-industrial countries like those in South America, the newly-independent countries of Asia and, later, Africa. Their roles have since evolved considerably, with the IMF now primarily arranging "bailouts" for countries in crisis and making heavily-conditioned loans to low-income countries. The World Bank has added similar policy-based loans to its agenda while continuing to fund large infrastructure projects such as dams, power plants, and roads.

The World Bank Group now consists of five entities, the largest of which remains the IBRD, which makes loans to governments for large infrastructure projects.

The International Finance Corporation (IFC), founded in 1956, makes loans to or invests in private companies operating

Graphic courtesy Third World First - BRIC

in borrowing countries. The International Development Association (IDA), founded in 1960, makes long-term low-interest loans, to the most impoverished countries in the world. The Multilateral Guarantee Investment Agency (MIGA), founded in 1988, provides political risk insurance to corporations undertaking projects in the developing world. Finally, the International Center for the Settlement of Investment Disputes (ICSID) serves as a tribunal to settle disputes between governments and corporations. Though not an officially separate entity, the World Bank also hosts the Global Environment Facility (GEF), created as a result of the 1992 "Earth Summit" in Rio de Janeiro, Brazil to make loans for environmentally-sustainable development programs.

Decision-Making

The IMF and World Bank frequently defend their projects, practices, and policies by pointing to their status as multilateral organizations, controlled by the governments of the world (almost all of which are members). The institutions' Board of Governors, which meets twice a year, consists of the finance ministers or central bank governors of every member country. Those meetings, however, are a forum for speech-making, rather than deliberation over the institutions' policies. The Governors' ratification of the institutions' procedures amounts to a ceremonial event — more like a graduation than an examination.

Decisions about the policies, loans, and operations of the World Bank and IMF are in fact made by the respective Boards of Directors of each institution. Those Boards meet in continuous session (usually three sessions per week) at the Washington headquarters. Each Board has 24 members, some of whom represent one country (in the cases of the U.S., Japan, Germany, France, the U.K., China, Russia, and Saudi Arabia), and others representing groups of as many as 27 countries (eg. Africa).

The apportionment of voting power calls into question the assertion that the institutions are representative and democratic. Each country is assigned a voting ratio proportional to the size of its economy, which also determines the size of its contributions (expressed as shares) to the institutions.

Both the World Bank and the IMF are set up so that each member country gets 250 votes to start. Above and beyond this base amount, a country earns one additional vote for each share of stock held. Out of the 184 member countries, the U.S. holds 16.4% of the Bank's voting power, with 265,219 votes and 17.10% of the voting power in the IMF. The next largest shareholder is Japan with 127,250 votes, or 7.87% of the Bank's overall voting power and 6.14% of the IMF's voting power, less than half the votes of the U.S. If we were to combine the voting power of the five largest shareholder countries by adding in Germany, France, and the U.K., their voting power would equal 604,412 votes or 37.38% of the overall vote in the Bank and in the IMF they would control 39.14%. Canada and Italy are parts of country groups, like most other member countries. They usually name the groups 'lead representative,' so that together, the G7 countries control over 45% of the votes in both institutions.

In comparison, the country with the lowest percentage of voting power, Palau, holds only 266 votes — .02% of the Bank's total, and even less in the IMF. The combined voting power of the 100 smallest shareholders in the Bank equals a mere 6.54%, more than 2.5 times less than the power of the United States' share. As a consequence, sub-Saharan Africa, the region most heavily patrolled by the IMF and World Bank, has just two members on the Boards, each of whom represent over 20 countries, and who together cast 4.59% of the votes at the IMF and 5.35% of the votes at the Bank.

Major policy decisions at either institution require a "super-majority" vote of 85%. The United States has made clear that it will not permit its share to fall below 15%, meaning it will continue to hold de facto veto power at the IMF and World Bank indefinitely.

In addition, by unwritten custom, the President of the United States selects the President of the World Bank, and the countries of Western Europe choose the Managing Director of the IMF. The concentration of power in the hands of the U.S. and a few other wealthy countries was considered necessary to keep the institutions funded.

Members

184 countries are members of both the IMF and the World Bank. The membership expanded considerably in the early 1990s, when the countries of the former Soviet Union and its satellites rejoined after leaving decades before. Only seven countries, and only three with populations of appreciable size, are not members: Andorra, Cuba, North Korea, Liechtenstein, Nauru, Taiwan, and Tuvalu. ■

FOR FURTHER INFORMATION:

www.imf.org
www.worldbank.org

Jubilee USA Network • Washington, DC USA

Debt siphons resources from health care, education and other vital services to pay off wealthy nations and creditors. New loans to pay the debt create an unending "debt treadmill" and are heavily conditioned on economic reform measures — "structural adjustment" — that deepen poverty.

By the early 1980s, many developing countries had accumulated massive debt burdens. It was the threat of defaults to large private banks — which, in the case of the largest Latin American economies (Mexico, Brazil, and Argentina) threatened to create global chaos — that spurred both the first modern-day "bailouts" and the widespread introduction of structural adjustment programs (whose conditions, at any rate, are similar to those routinely attached to bailout loans). With the debts to private banks effectively transformed into public debt (to the IMF and World Bank), the debt crisis receded from world headlines, but never loosened its grip on Southern countries. The epidemic of structural adjustment programs it spawned led the Global South into the system of corporate globalization.

In the mid-1990s, anti-debt campaigns from around the world came together to form the Jubilee movement, calling for comprehensive cancellation of impoverished country debt by 2000. The IMF and World Bank responded in 1996 with the Heavily Indebted Poor Country (HIPC) debt initiative, which has proven to be slow, insufficient, and as burdened with harmful conditions as the original loans. While the G7 responded to the Jubilee movement's pressure in 1999 by "enhancing" the initiative, the program was never

HELLO, IS THAT THE DEVELOPED WORLD? LISTEN, WE CAN'T START CONSTRUCTION TILL YOU REMOVE WHAT YOU LEFT ON OUR SITE.

meant to cancel debt so much as to reduce it to an arbitrarily-determined "sustainable" level and further lock governments in to the lend-and-pay cycle. The U.S., along with several other G7 countries, did pledge (and follow through) to cancel the debts directly owed to them by the most impoverished countries.

Even with HIPC in place, however, the debt crisis continues to worsen. The World Bank has, in 2002 and 2003, published reports that acknowledge the failure of HIPC and the exaggerated expectations it encouraged at the time of its debut.

Where some funds have been freed up by debt reduction programs, they have made a substantial difference. Savings from debt relief have:

- More than doubled school enrollment in Uganda;
- Vaccinated half a million children against fatal diseases in Mozambique;
- Provided three extra years of schooling for Honduran children; and
- Provided resources for the fight against HIV/AIDS in countries like Mali, Mozambique, Senegal and Cameroon.

Recent studies document that the debt relief delivered to date has resulted in increases in spending on education and health in Africa — and no increases in spending on defense. In some cases, health spending has increased by 70%, and education spending has grown by more than 140%. Imagine what complete debt cancellation would do to fight hunger and poverty!

In the period after 2000, Jubilee campaigns have expanded their vision beyond programs offered by the IMF and World Bank and promises made by wealthy governments. For most of them, the emphasis is now on more permanent solutions to the debt crisis. Campaigners are encouraging indebted governments to repudiate, or refuse to pay, their debts. They are also focusing on the dubious origins of much of the debt that Southern peoples are asked to pay, and demanding not only cancellation of illegitimate debts but reparations — payments from the North to the South — to compensate for centuries of exploitation and ecological damage. ■

FOR FURTHER INFORMATION:
www.jubileeusa.org

Since the late 1970s, the IMF and World Bank have played a decisive role in reshaping the economies of impoverished countries in order to fit them into the free market global economy. They have done so largely by requiring a series of macroeconomic policy reforms as conditions for obtaining new loans or debt relief. Other creditors followed the lead of the IMF, whose "seal of approval," necessary for a country to be considered credit-worthy, could only be gained by implementing these policy changes.

Often referred to as "structural adjustment," the essential nature and purpose of these economic policies, aggressively promoted by the IMF and the World Bank, endure regardless of what they are called or in which programs of the international financial institutions they are imbedded. They are intended first to stabilize economies in serious trouble with, for example, run-away inflation, and then to open, or liberalize, them.

Key structural adjustment measures include: privatization of government-owned enterprises, imposition of user fees and privatization of services, cuts in government spending, promotion of exports, trade liberalization, financial sector liberalization, higher interest rates, reforms in particular sectors like agriculture and mining, eliminating subsidies on consumer items such as food, fuel and medicines, labor market reforms, and tax increases.

Structural adjustment has wreaked havoc on impoverished communities as access to affordable, basic services has become much more difficult; women and children have been especially hard hit. For years, IMF-required cuts in government spending have immediately cut food and transportation subsidies and reduced the basic services available to the poor. More recently, some efforts have been made to protect spending on health care and education.

The failure of small and medium sized businesses following competition from cheap, subsidized imports and the withdrawal of sources of credit; the destruction of small-scale and subsistence farming with the emphasis on production for export; labor market reforms, and lay-offs following privatization or civil-service reform: these have all resulted in higher levels of unemployment and underemployment. In addition, real wages have deteriorated, income distribution has become less equitable and workers' rights and unions have been weakened.

As just one example of the impact of structural adjustment, a report published in 2002 by the Structural Adjustment Participatory Review Initiative Network (SAPRIN) finds that "In Ecuador, open

unemployment more than doubled under adjustment from 6% in the late 1980s to 14.4% in 1999. The poorest 20% of the population saw unemployment rates rise from 10 to 24%, while the situation of the richest 20% remained unchanged at less than 5%."

Structural adjustment also contributes to environmental degradation through its aggressive promotion of exports to generate foreign exchange, especially agricultural products and mineral resources, as well as through its weakening of environmental regulations. Countries often over-exploit their resources through unsustainable forestry, mining and agricultural practices that generate pollution and environmental destruction.

As SAPRIN concludes, "The intransigence of international policymakers as they continue their prescription of structural adjustment policies is expanding poverty, inequality and insecurity around the world. [...] Their effects, particularly on the poor, are so profound and pervasive that no amount of targeted social investments can begin to address the social crises that they have engendered." ∎

FOR FURTHER INFORMATION:

www.saprin.org
www.maryknoll.org

Focus on the Global South • Bangkok THAILAND

The Poverty Reduction Strategy Paper (PRSP), introduced at the 1999 annual meetings of the IMF and World Bank, is the World Bank's new name for its structural adjustment programs (SAPs). A PRSP comes twinned with the Poverty Reduction Growth Facility (PRGF), which is the International Monetary Fund's (IMF) new name for SAPs. In order to qualify for concessional loans from the World Bank and IMF, all low-income countries must prepare a PRSP and agree to the PRGF.

In theory, a PRSP is supposed to be a document prepared by a national government, with the advice of World Bank and IMF staff, that identifies the incidence and causes of poverty, who the poor are, and strategies for overcoming poverty, including policy and expenditure targets. It is supposed to be "locally generated and owned," developed through "wide participatory dialogue," and focused at both the micro and macro policy-making levels. The PRSP is expected to "encourage the accountability of governments to their own people and domestic constituencies rather than to external funders," whereby, "the poor become active participants, not just passive recipients." *[All quotations are from IMF and World Bank documents.]*

PRSP policy conditions are essentially identical to those imposed by SAPs...

Although the World Bank and IMF adopted the new names and language in 1999, they have yet to prove that the PRSP and PRGF are different from traditional SAPs. Experiences from Asia, Africa and Latin America show that governments have little control over the structure, content and policy prescriptions in PRSPs. The success of a PRSP is judged by how rapidly and intensively a government can impose IMF-dictated macroeconomic policies and World Bank-dictated structural reforms.

At the heart of all PRSPs are "policy matrices," which are lists of policy conditions that countries must fulfill if they want low-interest loans. These include: fiscal austerity; privatization of public utilities and services; opening up the country to foreign trade and investment; "harmonizing" trade and investment policies with WTO agreements; shrinking government capacity; expanding the role of the private sector; removing government controls over services, markets, and private sector operations (also called deregulation or liberalization); imposing user fees for essential services such as water, health and education (also called cost recovery), cutting public subsidies for the poor and vulnerable, and supporting rapid, export-led economic growth. Not only are these policy conditions essentially identical to those imposed through SAPs, but the same conditions also appear in

PRSPs from every different region — Asia-Pacific, Africa, and Latin America and the Caribbean.

PRSPs have quickly become the main policy framework through which the world's major donors relate to low-income countries. Without a World Bank and IMF approved PRSP, a low-income country is likely to be virtually cut off from international aid, trade and finance. The US, European Union, Japan, Canada, Australia and other wealthy donor countries have fully endorsed the PRSP-PRGF framework, and many have agreed to co-finance parts of PRSP-PRGF programs.

The IMF has yet to show conclusive links between its macroeconomic conditionalities and poverty elimination; indeed, a report published by the IMF in March 2003 confesses that "globalization" policies prescribed by the international financial institutions frequently hurt the poor. Despite the rhetoric of "nationally-driven" development, the PRSP-PRGF framework conflicts with local and national development priorities and discourages popular participation in the formulation of national development policies.

Contrary to claims of "wide participation," PRSPs have not been developed through participatory processes. Participation has largely been limited to consultations with prominent and well-resourced NGOs on pre-prepared documents. Labor unions, workers' organisations, farmer and fisher groups, women's organizations, indigenous peoples' networks, medical associations and academics have not been included in the process. What participation has been allowed has been largely geared toward budget choices and gauging poverty; civil society is assumed to be uninterested or unqualified to be at the table when macroeconomic prescriptions (trade policy, liberalization, fiscal policy, etc.) are discussed.

At a meeting in Kampala, Uganda in 2001, over 40 African civil society organizations endorsed a declaration rejecting participation in the PRSP/PRGF process. In Pakistan, a broad coalition of NGOs, consumer rights groups, research institutes, unions, peasant and fisher-folk organisations, political parties, journalists and the Pakistan Human Rights Commission have formally rejected the content and process of the PRSP.

Concerned citizens in numerous Southern countries are learning about the PRSP and PRGF, and most see it as a ploy to make standard structural adjustment policies appear to be endorsed by civil society. The attempted subterfuge may well be backfiring. ∎

FOR FURTHER INFORMATION:

www.focusweb.net

Social Justice Committee • Montréal, Quebec CANADA

The Heavily Indebted Poor Countries (HIPC) debt initiative, the international community's main effort to address the ongoing debt crisis, does not achieve its main objective: a permanent exit for impoverished countries from the burden of debt.

Specific flaws in the program include:

- Low relief levels: Debt relief payments by countries that have completed the program, and by countries with programs underway, continue to be a substantial drain on their economies, stunting efforts at productive development.

- Snail's pace: The program is very slow, producing only seven graduates out of more than forty candidates since it was launched in 1996.

- Conditionalities: HIPC is laden with conditions, primarily generic economic reform programs that have failed to produce economic growth results while failing to shield the vulnerable.

- Redirection of funds: Debt is often not actually cancelled, but the money is put into special accounts with restrictions on how it can be spent. Only one country has been able to get its hands on the full amount that is supposed to be available from debt "cancellation."

As the main creditor to impoverished countries, the World Bank accounts for a substantial amount of both HIPC countries' older debts and new lending. The Bank, however, has refused to consider full cancellation of those debts, even though the G7 countries have all adopted that position. It is also engaged in actively promoting new borrowing throughout the South, without adequate oversight or accountability to the people who will inherit the debts created.

Every country seeking HIPC debt relief must comply with an IMF program of economic restructuring, or structural adjustment as it is more commonly known. This usually includes cuts in spending, the sale of state enterprises to private owners, and layoffs in the public sector.

Of the twenty countries eligible for relief, up to half are substantially "off-track" with their adjustment programs and thus are not making progress to the HIPC "completion point." Countries must reach the completion point in order to qualify for the full debt relief they are eligible for.

Honduras, for example, is stalled in the HIPC Initiative in large part because the financial institutions believe that the government is paying teachers too much. Senegal's delays relate to public spending and the slow process of privatizing its peanut production. Guyana is delayed because of public spending and the slow process of privatizing sugar production.

The World Bank and IMF consistently argue that they do not have the resources necessary to write off the debts of the poorest countries without imperiling their operations and credit rating. But reluctance to consider full cancellation of multilateral debt is due more to political and ideological factors than economic ones. The World Bank is the largest single creditor to impoverished countries, but much of its money is loaned to middle-income countries for purposes other than poverty reduction, or invested in private-sector projects as an incentive to attract investors. If the World Bank truly believed its motto -- "our dream is a world free of poverty" -- it would re-order its priorities to provide the comprehensive debt cancellation required for the elimination of poverty and progress in economic development. ■

FOR FURTHER INFORMATION:
www.socialjusticecommittee.org

FALSE START: THE IMF'S SOVEREIGN DEBT RESTRUCTURING MECHANISM

Halifax Initiative • Whitehorse, Yukon Territory CANADA

International debt management since the 1980s has been characterized by fragmented and inadequate efforts by creditors to restructure or reduce debt, resulting in increasingly unpayable debt burdens in developing countries.

At its 2003 Spring Meeting, the International Monetary Fund (IMF) discussed a new mechanism to restructure the debt of middle-income countries. This mechanism, known as the Sovereign Debt Restructuring Mechanism (SDRM), would allow private creditors to negotiate a restructuring arrangement with a debtor government that is insolvent or approaching insolvency.

The proposal responds to factors including:

■ recurrent financial crises resulting in sovereign default or near default (Argentina);

■ increasingly large and ineffective "bailouts" of private creditors (East Asia, Russia, Brazil, Turkey);

■ the rise in influence of minority creditors and their claims against sovereign debtors.

With the SDRM proposal, the IMF is attempting to limit massive bailout payments, which have drained its coffers, and regain international credibility lost through its mishandling of recent financial crises.

The response to the SDRM proposal has been vocal and critical. The private sector strongly opposes any plan that might force it to take a write-down on its debt. The response of civil society has become uniformly negative as the SDRM proposal has evolved.

The SDRM reflects much of what is wrong with the current state of international debt management and is an unacceptable solution to the external debt burden faced by insolvent middle-income countries. Rather than benefiting from the lessons learned through its flawed Heavily Indebted Poor Countries (HIPC) initiative designed to reduce poorest country debt, the IMF has effectively created a copy of it with the SDRM – a "Massively Indebted Middle Income Country" (MIMIC)

ANOTHER I.M.F. RECIPE FOR FAILURE

initiative. The SDRM mimics the HIPC initiative with additional provisions that further weaken debtor interests and enhance the authority of the IMF acting on behalf of private sector creditors.

The SDRM:

- Is biased towards creditors in violation of the concepts of fair and impartial treatment to achieve a just and viable solution. The SDRM does not aim to cancel the debt in the interest of a sustainable exit from debt, but merely to restructure in the interests of creditors;

- Exempts the IMF and World Bank from the restructuring process, thus creating unequal burden-sharing between creditors and the resultant inability to achieve a comprehensive solution. The IMF is the very "rogue creditor" a viable debt restructuring mechanism would address;

- Requires that all participant countries adhere to IMF-imposed structural adjustment policies as a condition of debt restructuring;

- Effectively concedes to the IMF the role of determining what level of debt will be deemed "sustainable." Under the HIPC initiative, the IMF has been widely criticized for overestimating the debt load a country is capable of carrying in order to minimize creditor costs to cancel debt;

- Fails to recognize or address the illegitimacy of debts and therefore the responsibility of creditors who lend imprudently and the right of citizens to refuse to pay illicit loans;

- Makes no provisions to protect domestic budgetary resources for the poor;

- Seeks to re-legitimize and expand the influence of the IMF in global economic financial governance through changes to the IMF's Articles of Agreement creating a new legal entity and expanded conditionality requirements;

- Fails to engage the public on whose behalf debt was contracted or to guarantee basic budget protection. This is profoundly anti-democratic.

What IMF officials and governments were not discussing at their Spring Meetings is a proposal, advanced by civil society, known as the Fair and Transparent Arbitration Process (FTAP). The FTAP proposal would provide a neutral forum for the resolution of insolvency that respects and balances the rights of debtor and creditor. At its core, the FTAP seeks to transform the existing unjust balance of power between international finance and debtor nations and their people. For the first time, creditor interests would be addressed only after the fundamental human rights of people in debtor nations are assured. The FTAP would also have the power to determine the illegitimacy of debt and annul it.

The FTAP aims for a comprehensive solution to insolvency and is therefore inclusive of all forms of debt – private sector, bilateral and multilateral. Because the IMF would only be one creditor among many, the FTAP would effectively reduce its influence in international debt management and avoid the conflict of interest inherent in the SDRM.

The FTAP offers equal and comprehensive treatment, impartial arbitration, treatment of illegitimate debt and a commitment to debtor viability. It ensures basic protection of human rights and human dignity. It would also set the stage for a full hearing on reparation for exploited countries. Meaningful long-term resolution of the global debt crises demands nothing less. ■

FOR FURTHER INFORMATION:
www.halifaxinitiative.org

The World Bank's International Development Association: Developing Whom?

Halifax Initiative • Ottawa, Ontario CANADA

The International Development Association (IDA) is the tentacle of the World Bank that provides financing to low-income countries. It grew out of efforts by countries of the Global South during the 1950s to establish a Special UN Fund for Economic Development. "SUNFED," as it was known, was to have been controlled by the United Nations. Global North countries, led by the United States, resisted these efforts and eventually proposed a soft loan affiliate at the World Bank (IDA). Since its founding in 1960, IDA has made very-low-interest, long-term loans totaling about $120 billion to 106 countries.

In practice it is often hard to distinguish IDA policies and practices from those of the "main" part of the World Bank, the International Bank for Reconstruction and Development (IBRD). IDA shares its Board of Directors, President and staff with the IBRD. The differences come in the terms of the loans made — IDA loans charge about .5% interest and are payable over 40 years — and in the source of the money: IDA funds come from bilateral contributions from donors rather than through the sale of World Bank bonds on international capital markets.

IDA loans have contributed to the on-going debt crisis of the poorest countries. Using even the very narrow criteria of the Heavily Indebted Poor Country (HIPC) Initiative, 41 of 79 current IDA-eligible countries were identified as having debt burdens that compromise the country's capacity for development and growth.

AN EXPANDING FREE MARKET EXTENDS ALL BELLIES

In the most recent negotiations among donors to determine IDA funding levels, completed in 2002, the Bush Administration pushed a proposal to make 50% of IDA's future programs grants rather than loans. The final compromise reached calls for between 18 and 21% of IDA financing to be grant-based, and there are suspicions that much of the grant money will subsidize privatization of essential services.

While the debate over grants delayed the IDA agreement for several months, debt cancellation for the heavily indebted IDA borrowers was never discussed.

There is little justification for maintaining IDA as part of the World Bank Group. In over 40 years, IDA has not demonstrated any special capacity for dealing with the problems of low-income countries; indeed, following the standard World Bank policies has exacerbated poverty and social inequality in IDA borrowers. The idea of separating IDA from the World Bank Group, either making it a free-standing agency or a part of the United Nations, can no longer be ignored. The U.S. government's success in 1960 in preventing the Global South from having a greater measure of control over the agency with the greatest resources for the poorest countries should at last be reversed. A divorce from the World Bank would be a significant step forward for self-determination and democracy in the development process. ■

FOR FURTHER INFORMATION:
www.halifaxinitiative.org

THE INTERNATIONAL FINANCE CORPORATION

50 Years Is Enough Network • Washington, DC USA

The International Finance Corporation (IFC) was established in 1956 as part of the World Bank Group, with a mission "to promote private sector investment in developing countries, which will reduce poverty and improve peoples' lives."

The IFC fulfills its mandate through investment in large infrastructure projects, and direct financing of private corporations operating in the developing world. The IFC has come under steady criticism for directing 85% of its investment resources to 15 countries that could attract investment without the security provided by an inflow of public resources, as well as to multinational corporations such as Citigroup and Exxon/Mobil.

The focus on a narrow range of countries — despite the IFC's mission to encourage investment in economies otherwise passed over — can be attributed to the requirement that all of the IFC's investments make a profit. This criterion eliminates consideration of many development projects that would most benefit the poor.

Although it is part of the World Bank Group, the IFC resists adopting policies on the environment, indigenous peoples, resettlement, and information disclosure developed by the IBRD, arguing that such rules must be adapted to protect business "confidentiality" and "trade secrets." This has created obstacles to using the leverage the IFC commands to require higher standards — an ironic development, given that the IFC boasts that its involvement has the effect of increasing the quality of private-sector projects.

The IFC often becomes involved in projects after key decisions have already been made, thus diminishing its "consultation and environmental assessment processes" to an after-the-fact rationalization process for a predetermined project design. In Chile, for example, the IFC supported the Pangue hydroelectric dam on the Bio-Bio River, but failed to sufficiently assess the impact that the project would have on indigenous peoples and environment. As a result, countless families were forced to relocate to make way for the dam. In Kyrgyzstan, the IFC is participating in a mining project with a large Canadian corporation. After the first two years of operation, the mine had already caused three serious toxic spills, including one which spilled two tons of cyanide into the Barksoon River, an important source of drinking water and irrigation for local communities. In both countries, basic information was denied to not only the general public, but to the project-affected communities as well. In fact, the IFC continues to withhold emergency plans for the Kyrgyz mine to the local communities.

One of the best-known recent IFC projects is the Chad-Cameroon Pipeline Project, one of the largest private sector investments in Africa. The IFC has directly invested $400 million in this project and has facilitated additional funding of $1.3 billion from commercial lenders and international capital markets. This financial support was provided despite the fact that the IFC's own risk assessment process concluded that the project's risk level was "significant" and posed potentially "significant adverse impacts" including ecological destruction, restricted access to clean water, loss of fertile land, increased risk of ethnic conflict, and increased incidence of HIV/AIDS in zones near project facilities. Perhaps most ominous was the prospect of providing valuable support to two of the most notoriously corrupt and anti-democratic regimes in Africa. And indeed, the first payment of nearly $5 million to the Chadian government was immediately redirected to the purchase of weapons for use in attacking the country's perennial rebel groups. The World Bank was able to use its influence to end the detention of opposition candidates, but the dictator's grip in the end has been strengthened by the oil project.

The IFC is primarily a vehicle of "corporate welfare" and would better serve its ostensible beneficiaries if its investments were liquidated and the proceeds used to fund reparations for the impact of over 50 years of World Bank and IFC projects. ■

MIGA: TAXPAYER-FUNDED PROFIT INSURANCE FROM THE WORLD BANK

50 Years Is Enough Network • Washington, DC USA

The Multilateral Investment Guarantee Agency (MIGA) was created in 1988 as part of the World Bank Group. Its mission is the promotion of foreign direct investment into emerging economies, with the avowed aim of bringing about poverty reduction and an improved standard of living. MIGA approaches this goal by offering political risk insurance (guarantees) to investors and lenders.

MIGA's strategies fail to specifically target poverty reduction, instead working under the assumption that any economic growth, regardless of its distribution, will benefit the poor. Most of MIGA's coverage is offered to multinational corporations, opening it up to charges of corporate welfare from many quarters, including the U.S. Congress, which regularly reduces or refuses its annual funding request. Within a five year period MIGA has provided more than $220 million in political risk insurance to Citibank, more than $150 million to Exxon, Elf (the largest French oil company), and BP (British Petroleum), $60 million to Coca Cola and Pepsi, and over $13 million to Radisson and Marriot luxury hotels. Giant corporations working on non-essential projects are the recipients of the majority of MIGA's resources while the small and medium-sized

In the name of "investor confidence," MIGA uses public funds to guarantee profits for multinational corporations.

enterprises that create jobs and re-invest their earnings locally — and that MIGA publicizes the most — can take advantage of only a small portion.

When claims must be paid to these corporations, it is the citizens of both the borrowing countries and the creditor countries who take on much of the financial responsibility. In the late 1990s MIGA paid over $15 million to Enron under the breach-of-contract provision for a power project in Indonesia that was postponed due to the Asian financial crisis. MIGA, in turn, received a corresponding payment from the Indonesian government — even though no power project was completed and Enron incurred no losses. (Enron, of course, has since been exposed as a master of making money out of thin air.)

MIGA claims it requires investors to adhere to rigid social and environmental standards, but in fact it is not required to, and usually does not, subject itself to the system of checks and balances that the other parts of the World Bank do. In addition, MIGA often refuses to release basic information to project-affected communities, not only in the project-planning stages but also in the event of project failure, especially those resulting in environmental catastrophe. Reports used by the Board of Directors to predict the safety and success of possible projects are deemed confidential. Once projects are approved, the level of transparency remains low. Environmental and social monitoring reports, and even emergency response plans and evaluations, are routinely denied to the public.

MIGA is widely considered the most vulnerable part of the World Bank Group — not just because of hostility in the U.S. Congress, but because private insurers now offer nearly identical services. In its quest to find a distinctive function to justify its continuation as a publicly-funded organization, MIGA has considered a wide range of possibilities. Among the most alarming of these ideas is that of offering insurance to corporations that might be confronted with consumer boycotts. For example, were this proposal to be adopted, the World Bank could insure apparel companies against the economic effects of consumer campaigns designed to raise awareness of the exploitation of sweatshop labor.

There are few things more dangerous than a bureaucracy in search of a function. MIGA's role from the beginning has been to insure corporate profits, and it looks as if it could get worse. MIGA's disintegration could not come soon enough. ■

Workers have been among the primary victims of more than two decades of structural adjustment policies (SAPs) promoted by the IMF and World Bank. Pressure by the international financial institutions' (IFIs) on developing and former Soviet-bloc countries to privatize state-owned enterprises and squeeze public spending has resulted in massive job losses, declining wages and deteriorating working conditions throughout most of these countries. The promised growth of private-sector jobs that was supposed to absorb the workers who lost their jobs after the downsizing of the state never materialized.

As a result of these policies, formal unemployment rates have increased throughout the South. But an even larger number of workers have been pushed into the so-called informal economy, often at below minimum wages and without any form of social protection. It is estimated that a majority of employed workers in the Global South are now in the informal economy; the rates vary from about half of the urban workforce in Latin America to over two-thirds in Sub-Saharan Africa. Consequently, inequality levels in developing countries have been increasing sharply in the past two decades, and the gap between rich and poor within those countries has become much greater than in developed countries.

FALLOUT FROM THE NEW GLOBAL ECONOMY!

Rather than attempting to extend social protection to unprotected workers, or helping them organize so that they can campaign for improved labor standards, the IFIs have been pressuring developing countries to dismantle the limited protection of workers that they do have. In fact, "labor market flexibility" has been one of the pillars of the "Washington Consensus" policies of structural adjustment, along with privatization, reduction of the role of the state, and trade liberalization. The IFIs' rationale is that cheaper labor and more flexible hiring and firing rules will lead firms to increase their workforce. In reality, there is little evidence that these measures have done much more than drive wages and working conditions of the formal work force down towards the levels of unprotected workers. The kinds of measures that the IMF and World Bank have pressured countries to adopt range from reducing minimum wages in Bulgaria and Poland, to reducing severance pay in Colombia and Sri Lanka, and to eliminating seniority-based promotions in Mexico.

Both the IMF and World Bank have proclaimed in recent years that they support the International Labor Organization's (ILO) core labor standards: elimination of forced labor, child labor and discrimination; freedom of association and right to collective bargaining. However the IFIs' actions in pushing countries to ignore some of these rights often speak louder than their words of support. For example, the IFIs have been active in a number of countries to encourage governments to limit the scope of collective bargaining and to dismantle all forms of industry-wide bargaining. This has occurred, or is taking place, in Argentina, Chile, Croatia, Mexico and Pakistan, to name just a few countries.

*Rather than attempting to extend social protection to unprotected workers, or helping them organize so they can campaign for improved labor standards, the IFIs have been pressuring developing countries to dismantle the limited protection of workers that they **do** have.*

Once industry-wide bargaining is eliminated, the more vulnerable workers in small and medium enterprises in effect lose their access to collective bargaining rights.

In several countries, the IMF and World Bank have supported the creation of Export Processing Zones (EPZs), where multinational enterprises are exempted from having to abide by a number of laws intended to protect workers. As a general rule, freedom of association is severely restricted or altogether absent in the EPZs, of which there are currently some 3000 worldwide. A more recent trend is for the IFIs to pressure countries to extend the deregulated status accorded to firms in the EPZs to the entire economy, in this case all businesses in the country can end up as winners...and all workers as losers. ∎

FOR FURTHER INFORMATION:
www.icftu.org

In 1980 the United Nations (UN) reported that women constitute half of the world's population; perform nearly two-thirds its work hours; receive one tenth of the world's income; and own less than one-hundredth of the world's property. More recent UN data indicates that not much has changed. In the 21st century women still get short shrift. In developing nations two thirds of women's work is unpaid, compared to one quarter of men's work; women produce half the world's food but own only 1% of farmland; and in Africa, women produce 80% of the food but receive only 10% of the agricultural credit.

Overall, women comprise a majority of the world's poor, and are at particular risk in the globalized economy. Writing in the 50 Years Is Enough Network newsletter, *Economic Justice News*, Pamela Sparr has described persuasive evidence that gender-based oppression of women and girls lies at the heart of the functioning of the global economy, and specifically, of structural adjustment policies (SAPs). Often the gender analysis is centered on the fact (which the World Bank disputes) that the poor are disproportionately female and that SAPs have increased female poverty.

Women are now entering the workplace in increasing numbers, but their economic status is deteriorating. In the Report on the Progress of the World's Women 2000, the United Nations Development Fund for Women (UNIFEM) found that globalization intensifies the existing inequalities and insecurities to which poor women are subject.

The globalized economy depends on women's work in the service and industry sectors to assure continued growth and repayment of debts. Poor women continue to provide the low wage, manual labor, often under sub-standard working conditions, that attracts transnational companies to invest in their countries. But they don't reap the benefits of their hard work.

As Sparr notes, national governments saw low-wage labor as their comparative advantage (what they are best-positioned to provide) in international markets. They attracted foreign investors by opening export processing zones (EPZs) which provided tax holidays, infrastructure support, etc. As we know from the all-too-familiar images, this comparative advantage was built upon female labor from the women in Indonesia making Nike shoes to the women cultivating flowers in Kenya for shipment to European supermarkets to women in Salvadoran maquiladoras sewing designer label jeans for U.S. consumers. Factory owners often utilize gender-specific strategies to keep women workers in their place: mandatory "beauty contests," sexual harassment from supervisors, mandatory pregnancy testing, forced contraception, and sexual violence committed against women labor organizers.

Throughout the world, women:

- still experience an often significant gender gap in earnings;

- hold few management positions in business, or decision-making positions relative to the economy;

- have unequal access to credit which would enable them to start their own small businesses;

- face huge imbalances in the ownership, control and regulation of information technologies, and remain in the minority among users of technology such as the Internet; and

- continue to provide an unequal share of unpaid labor (child and elder care, domestic and agricultural work) upon which societies depend, whose provision through public agencies has been decimated by IMF/World Bank conditions and trade rules. This labor is rarely factored into the global economic equation.

Societies with the greatest gender equality experience the fastest growth, illustrating the critical link between equality and economic progress. If a wider range of people, including poor women, are to gain and if economies are to grow, globalization must be reshaped so that it is more people-centered and more accountable to women. ∎

FOR FURTHER INFORMATION:

www.genderandtrade.org

www.cscsisters.org

Since publishing "Financing Health Services in Developing Countries: An Agenda for Reform" in 1987, the World Bank has aimed to play a prominent role in global health reform. The World Bank insured that the "Agenda" would play an important role in developing countries, since its thrust was to develop standard conditions for health financing to be included in structural adjustment programs.

The notion of health care as a fundamental human right was essentially abandoned when the World Bank asserted that impoverished countries cannot afford to fund universal health care, so they ought not try. Instead they were advised to adopt a more efficient, market-based approach that makes health care a commodity available only to those who can afford its market prices.

When the IMF tells a country it must reduce public spending in order to get loans and credit, health ministries are among the first to get their budgets cut.

In 1993, the World Bank used its annual World Development Report to further articulate its market-driven designs for health care delivery and finance. That report, "Investing in Health," recognized that poverty is a threat to health, but did not address the issue of economic inequality and poor health. It stated that economic growth is a condition for good health, and that countries must first improve their economic growth rates before they can significantly increase spending on health.

When the IMF tells a country it must reduce public spending in order to get loans and credit, health ministries are among the first to get their budgets cut. The cumulative effect of 20 years of chronic underfunding is the dilapidated state of many public health systems today — a disaster as the HIV/AIDS crisis continues to accelerate. In an effort to improve government spending in health, the World Bank calls for trimming government spending by reducing services from comprehensive coverage to a narrowly selective, cost-effective approach or a new type of selective primary health care. This has resulted in the World Bank's promotion of "user fees" — having clinics and hospitals charge poor people fees for services that used to be free. These fees had the perverse effect of preventing or discouraging many from using clinics at all.

For instance, when the World Bank mandated that Kenya impose charges of US$2.15 for patients, at Nairobi's Special Treatment Clinic for Sexually Transmitted Diseases (STDs) it resulted in a decrease in attendance of 40% for men and 65% for women over a nine-month period. Failure to treat STDs can significantly increase the likelihood of transmission of HIV/AIDS. Similar results, drops in attendance of 35 to 60 percent, have been seen throughout the developing world. And in a January 2000 United Nations Children's Fund (UNICEF) paper: *Absorbing Social Shocks, Protecting Children and Reducing Poverty*, which quotes a study in Zambia, a researcher witnessed the arrival of a 14 year old boy at a hospital, suffering from acute malaria. His parents were unable to pay the registration fee of ZK300 (33 cents US) and the boy was turned away. The report added that, "within two hours the boy was brought back dead."

In what it calls "promoting diversity and competition in health services," the World Bank seeks to increase the role of private doctors and businesses to deliver and finance most of those government services that were once subsidized or provided free to the impoverished. This moves money out of the public health care system and into the private sector, further depriving the public health system of funding. It moves forward the process of privatization of most medical and health services, and prices many medical interventions beyond the reach of the poorest people.

The dismantling of public health systems has spurred the privatization of the health sector and the growth of private medical corporations and health insurance schemes. The World Bank proposes increased health insurance coverage for middle income countries where consumers are given a choice between public and private insurance, which also drives funds out of the public systems and into the private sector. The process separates those who are deemed profitable from those who are not. This means funds are not distributed according to need, as in the case of collective public funds, but rather according to individual consumer premiums, thus separating out the higher payers for the private sector while worsening the underfunded public systems.

This process is also being furthered inside the World Trade Organization's agreement on the trade in health care services currently under negotiation. While the IMF and World Bank loan conditions call for the public health services markets to be privatized in borrowing countries, the new rules in the General Agreement on Trade in Services (GATS) in the WTO would restrict and prohibit countries from adequately regulating these markets once they are privatized. Many of the same types of regulations long used by all of the industrialized countries to develop, support, and protect their public health systems would become illegal under new GATS rules, depriving impoverished countries of ever benefiting from them.

Despite the ongoing push by the World Bank, IMF, and WTO to further liberalization in health care, strong public resistance is challenging the idea of market-based health systems. Whereas the World Bank insists that higher economic growth rates should precede improvements in health, an important new report by the World Health Organization's Commission on Macroeconomics and Health demonstrates that increased spending on public health lays the foundation necessary for future economic growth. When will the World Bank join the consensus that health comes before profit? ∎

HIV/AIDS: WORLD'S WORST EPIDEMIC, FUELLED BY DEBT & IMF/WORLD BANK POLICIES

Africa Action • Washington, DC USA

HIV/AIDS is the worst health crisis the world has ever seen. Since its discovery two decades ago, more than 25 million people have died of AIDS. At present, there are more than 42 million people living with HIV/AIDS worldwide.

Africa is "ground zero" of the global AIDS pandemic. Home to just over 10% of the world's population, sub-Saharan Africa has more than 75% of the world's HIV/AIDS cases. While HIV/AIDS is a global threat to human security that does not respect borders, it is taking its most devastating toll in Africa. Africa's people have been most vulnerable because poverty and inadequate access to health care services have fueled the spread of HIV/AIDS. At the same time, the policies of the U.S. government and the practices of the World Bank and the IMF have blocked Africans' own initiatives to fight HIV/AIDS.

While many African countries succeeded in improving their health care systems in the first decades after independence, the intervention of the World Bank and IMF reversed this progress. Investments in health care by African governments in the 1960s and 1970s achieved improvements in key health indicators. However, health indicators throughout Africa have fallen dramatically over the past two decades as a result of the HIV/AIDS crisis and other poverty-related diseases. Africa's health care systems have been unable

to cope with the crisis because of economic policies imposed by the World Bank and IMF, forcing cutbacks in public health and reducing access to basic services. The result has been that much of the progress made in Africa's early post-independence years has been undone. Average life expectancy in Africa has fallen by 15 years in just the past decade. AIDS is now the leading cause of death in sub-Saharan Africa.

As African countries struggle to cope with the impact of HIV/AIDS, their efforts are undermined by the massive amounts of money they must pay to foreign creditors each year. Africa currently spends $15 billion a year in debt servicing, according to the United Nations, yet Sub-Saharan Africa needs $10 billion a year to effectively fight the HIV/AIDS pandemic. The U.S. and other rich country governments, and the World Bank and IMF, continue to insist that African governments repay old, illegitimate debts to them, even while these debts divert desperately-needed resources from spending on health care and on the fight against HIV/AIDS. Despite creditors' promises of debt relief, most African governments still spend more money each year on debt service than on health care for their own people. Africa's burden of illegitimate external debt is a major obstacle to the continent's efforts to defeat HIV/AIDS.

Inadequate access to essential treatment and care also hinders the fight against HIV/AIDS in Africa. At present, only 1% of those living with HIV/AIDS in Africa have access to life-saving drugs that have cut death rates so dramatically in the U.S. and elsewhere. While the prohibitive cost of anti-AIDS drugs and the restrictive trade rules that have kept them out of reach for Africans have come under challenge recently, huge obstacles to treatment access still remain. The U.S. government continues to support the efforts of the big pharmaceutical companies to keep their profits high, at the expense of African lives. Its policies block African governments' efforts to acquire affordable medicines, including generic drugs, through entirely legal international trade provisions, such as compulsory licensing and parallel imports.

Throughout Africa, organizations and activists are struggling to prevent the spread of HIV/AIDS and to provide care to those already living with the disease. But their efforts are hindered by international obstacles and by insufficient resources. The recently established Global Fund to fight HIV/AIDS can provide the necessary support to effective prevention and treatment programs in Africa and other poor regions. However, the crucial work of the Global Fund is being undermined by inadequate funding from the U.S. and other rich countries.

HIV/AIDS is the greatest global threat that exists today, and the pandemic is still in its infancy. The continued spread of this disease threatens the future of entire economies and countries, and has serious implications for global stability. International inequalities and global racism have defined the pattern of the HIV/AIDS pandemic and continue to circumscribe the global response. The war on AIDS can still be won. But victory will depend on a successful effort to respond to the crisis first and foremost in Africa, the epicenter of the pandemic. ∎

FOR FURTHER INFORMATION:

www.africaaction.org

Essential Action • Washington, DC USA

For millions of HIV-infected people, there is a crying need to make lifesaving drugs more available—and quickly. Despite some real success in pressuring pharmaceutical companies to reduce prices for relatively new drugs, the "drug cocktail" used to treat HIV/AIDS in the United States remains far out of reach for all but a small handful of the growing African population with HIV/AIDS, now totaling more than 30 million.

A vital tool to help achieve affordability of essential medicines is compulsory licensing. Compulsory licensing enables a government to instruct a patent holder to license the right to use its patent to a company, government agency, or other party. Zimbabwe, for example, could issue a license to a local company for an HIV/AIDS drug manufactured by Bristol-Myers Squibb. The Zimbabwean firm would then manufacture the drug for sale in Zimbabwe under a generic name, and it would pay a reasonable royalty to Bristol-Myers Squibb on each sale.

Compulsory licensing lowers prices to consumers by creating competition in the market for the patented good. Its impact is similar to the introduction of generic competition at the end of a drug's patent term — prices come tumbling down. It can lower the price of medicines by 95% or more, and is permitted under the Agreement on Trade-Related Aspects of Intellectual Property Rights (TRIPS), administered by the World Trade Organization (WTO). It is regularly used in industrialized countries, including the U.S.

In the 1990s, working to protect the brand-name pharmaceutical industry, the United States placed significant bilateral pressure on countries not to engage in compulsory licensing. By the end of the decade, however, under pressure from AIDS and public health activists, the Clinton Administration retreated from its longstanding aggressive opposition to developing country efforts to undertake compulsory licensing.

The Bush administration has continued the revised Clinton policy but, like the Clinton administration, continues to pose serious obstacles to effective utilization of this crucial policy.

In 2001, at the Doha ministerial meeting of the WTO, countries pledged to rectify an irrational TRIPS provision that would particularly undermine a developing country's ability to institute effective compulsory licensing. Although TRIPS rules permit a country to assign a drug import license to a manufacturer outside the country, the licensee must have both permission to produce the drug in the country where its factory is based and permission to export the drug from that country. Thus, even if Zambia were to issue a compulsory drug license to a manufacturer in Canada, the Canadian manufacturer would be blocked from producing and exporting the drug if a brand-name company had a patent for that drug in Canada. Once patent protection is fully implemented in India in 2005, the effect of this provision will be to block compulsory licensing in markets that are not big enough to justify investment in manufacturing.

A special declaration on public health at the Doha ministerial obligated TRIPS members to address this problem in 2002. The United States along with the European Union, however, has blocked agreement on a workable solution. All parties recognize that some kind of exception to the irrational TRIPS provision is needed. The United States and EU have worked aggressively to limit the scope of the exception, with the United States going so far as to say it should apply only to infectious diseases.

Meanwhile, the United States is also working in diverse international trade negotiating fora to increase the monopoly protections afforded by patents and to diminish the ability of countries to initiate compulsory licensing and take steps to lower drug prices. For example, the U.S.-Jordan Free Trade Agreement, completed in fall 2000, and the U.S.-Chile and U.S.-Singapore free trade agreements, which are to be finally approved in 2003, sharply limit the grounds for compulsory licensing.

The U.S. is pursuing a similar negotiating strategy for the intellectual property portion of the proposed Free Trade Agreement of the Americas (FTAA), a trade agreement that would cover all of the Western hemisphere except for Cuba. The U.S. FTAA proposals include a variety of measures that would effectively extend patent terms, interfere with compulsory licensing, and otherwise undermine efforts by poor countries to make medicines more accessible.

Generally, the inclusion of intellectual property provisions in multiple-country trade agreements (like the FTAA) makes it much harder to ratchet down international patent protection obligations. Even if changes were made so that the WTO TRIPS agreement became less restrictive, for example, this move would have little impact on countries that had separate intellectual property obligations if they were equivalent to or more severe than the WTO mandates under the FTAA or other international trade agreements. ■

FOR FURTHER INFORMATION:

www.essentialaction.org

There are over 115 million children throughout the world who do not attend any form of schooling, and, as a result, are likely to join the over 860 million illiterate adults in the world. This educational crisis has recently been acknowledged by the international community which has responded by setting a "Millennium Development Goal" of universal access to primary education by 2015. However, many feel that the steps necessary to achieve this goal are being neglected and that this crisis, which is tied to lack of financial funding and debt, continues to be addressed with rhetoric which lacks sufficient financial backing. Africa especially finds itself at the epicenter of the global education crisis, with only 60% of its children receiving any formal education. Even those who do obtain formal education attend school for an average of just 3.5 years. The HIV/AIDS pandemic which is sweeping the continent increases the educational crisis, with more teachers dying of AIDS each year than there are new teachers being trained.

The World Bank boasts that it is the world's largest external funder of education. Until recently, however, it routinely recommended that countries employ "user fees" even for primary schooling. A 1998 World Bank internal report stated that 75% of projects in sub-Saharan Africa included the establishment or expansion of user fees. In Ghana, the Living Standards Survey for 1992-1993 found that 65% of rural families could not afford to send their children to school consistently due to user fees, and 77% of street children in the capital city of Accra had dropped out of school after the imposition of user fees. Inversely, according to the United Nations Children's Education

Fund (UNICEF), when Malawi eliminated a modest school fee in 1994, primary enrollment soared by 50% almost overnight, from 1.9 to 2.9 million students. In Malawi, the main beneficiaries were girls, who, in most countries, are the first to be withdrawn from school, and are traditionally the most negatively affected by user fees.

Only U.S. Congressional legislation, passed in 2000, has succeeded in focusing attention on the user fees policy scandal. That legislation requires that the US oppose any World Bank, IMF, or other multilateral development bank loan which includes user fees for basic health or education services. Even though the U.S. Treasury Department has been lax about implementing this rule, the signal sent by the bill was heard at the World Bank, which for the most part has reversed its policy on user fees for primary education. Yet despite the new bill, user fees have continued to be attached to loans in Ghana, Mauritania, and Burkina Faso (a country which has been identified as one of the fifteen countries facing the most dire of educational circumstances).

User fees, whether as part of a structural adjustment program or instituted "voluntarily" by a government, limit access to education. In the late 1990s, Nicaragua saw about a quarter of primary schoolchildren fail to enroll in primary school after charges for registration and a monthly stipend were introduced. In Niger, "cost recovery" (user fees) measures implemented as part of a structural adjustment program between 1986 and 1988 resulted in a sharp decline in already very low primary school enrollment rates, going from 28% in 1983 to 20% in 1988.

The World Bank and IMF further affect education indirectly through their refusal to grant comprehensive debt cancellation. Many countries spend more on debt repayments each year then they do on education and healthcare put together. In fact, each year Africa allocates $15 billion for debt repayments. According to Oxfam, if just $3.6 billion dollars of this money was annually redirected to education, all of Sub-Saharan Africa would be able to meet the 2015 goal of "education for all." Even the small amount of money generated by debt relief programs thus far has had obvious effects on the quality and access to education. For example, the reduction of a relatively small amount of debt in Uganda sparked a doubling in the school enrollment rates, and in Tanzania debt relief was followed by a 1.5 million increase in school enrollment in a matter of days. In neighboring Kenya, the promise of eliminating school fees was a key factor in the opposition's 2002 presidential election victory, and the implementation of the pledge has brought over one million new students into the system overnight. ∎

The lack of access to clean water is a growing global concern which has been exacerbated by the World Bank and IMF's international campaign to privatize water distribution. This water privatization strategy has further diminished the access to water in countries all over the world. South Africa is no exception.

The Freedom Charter adopted by the African National Congress (ANC) in 1955, which today's South African government still claims as its guiding manifesto, included a statement that "the national wealth of our country, the heritage of all South Africans, shall be restored to the people." Water has always been understood to be a right in the ANC's vision of South Africa.

The ANC's adoption of a World Bank-influenced, neo-liberal macroeconomic policy in 1996 made water (and all basic needs/services) a market commodity, to be bought and sold on the basis of private ownership and profit motive. Since then, South Africans have witnessed the gradual commercialization and privatization of water, a development that has increasingly been met with mass, organized resistance.

The swelling of citizen resistance is a pattern that has been mirrored in several other countries the World Bank has targeted for heavy pressure to privatize basic services in recent years. Ghana, the Philippines, Peru, Bolivia, and Paraguay are among the countries where activists have successfully organized to limit the progress of privatization.

The privatization of water began in earnest when the ANC government, acting on World Bank advice, halted subsidies and other financial support to municipal councils. This forced those councils to turn towards commercialization and privatization of basic services. The immediate result was massive increases in the price of water – by an astronomical 55% in Johannesburg — that hit poor communities the hardest.

Taking on board the World Bank's advice to introduce a "credible threat of cutting service," the Johannesburg council began cutting off water to tens of thousands of people who couldn't pay the increased prices. The "full cost recovery" model of the IFIs — i.e., no public subsidies to supplement user fees — has also resulted in tens of thousands of poor people being evicted from their homes. In Johannesburg alone, nearly 100,000 people suffered from water and electricity cut-offs during the first half of 2002, and the numbers continue to increase. Nationally, the privatization program of the ANC government has mandated water cut-offs for over ten million South Africans and home evictions for another two million for not paying water bills.

"We're here to serve!"
Make a PROFIT

Besides the cut-offs and evictions, the privatization of water in South Africa has resulted in several massive outbreaks of cholera. Not long after the French water giant Suez took over Johannesburg's water supply, an outbreak of cholera in the township of Alexandra affected thousands of poor families. The last two years have also seen the introduction of pre-paid water meters as another means to effect 'cost recovery' and limit the already minimal access to water for the poor.

The Anti-Privatisation Forum, alongside other social movements, has mobilized and organized poor communities in resistance. Educational and legal initiatives have been combined with regular mass struggle and have been aimed at empowering ordinary South Africans to reclaim the right to free basic services (water, electricity, education and housing). Community initiatives to bypass the pre-paid meter system, and thus regain degrees of community control, have been especially effective. While these struggles have not yet succeeded in reversing the privatization process, popular pressure has forced the ANC government to implement a partial free water policy. However, the scheme's free allocation of 6000 liters of water per household per month is completely insufficient for meeting even the basic sanitation requirements of the average poor household in South Africa. ■

FOR FURTHER INFORMATION:

www.apf.org.za

The stratification of land ownership has played a key role in creating and maintaining the massive discrepancies in wealth and the overall plague of poverty that faces much of the world today. Although this phenomenon has been common knowledge to some for decades now, others are just starting to admit to the correlation of land ownership and poverty. With the World Bank's acceptance of this reality and its introduction of land reform policies into many of their projects, the debate over what effective land reform looks like has re-emerged.

Although the World Bank's backing of land reform was crucial in shedding the "taboo" that once hobbled these policies, it has adopted a type of land reform which, like so many of its policies, benefits the wealthy while further marginalizing the poor. The World Bank's land reform policies fail to learn from the past, and reflect many of the poorly-conceived ideas of past failures.

The World Bank refers to its version of land reform as "market-based." The contradictions between ostensible goals and actual practice have quickly become apparent:

- When communal lands are titled in Mexico, Africa, and Asia, increases in individual competition often cause the breakdown of community-based resource management systems like terraces and small-scale irrigation, which leads to erosion and degradation.

- Land titling and free market land distribution can encourage land sell-offs, causing increased landlessness, migration to urban areas, and land concentration. This polarization of land ownership results in degradation of good soils as chemical-based strategies are adopted by export-oriented corporate farms.

- Under market-based land reform, landless farmers are offered loans to pay market prices for land. Landowners naturally find it more agreeable to get full payment right away than to have land expropriated with government agencies paying them over time or in bonds. These programs have failed to install adequate safeguards against landowners selling only marginal lands at unfair prices, or lands claimed by indigenous groups. Under such circumstances, cultivation can lead to deforestation, desertification, soil erosion, and the introduction of chemicals into fragile environments.

- Many of the land reform packages include production credits and technical assistance for export crops. Although support for new farms is fundamental to achieving successful land reform, the packages provided by Bank-funded programs are focused on

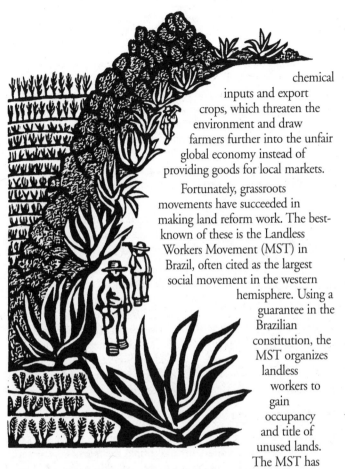

chemical inputs and export crops, which threaten the environment and draw farmers further into the unfair global economy instead of providing goods for local markets.

Fortunately, grassroots movements have succeeded in making land reform work. The best-known of these is the Landless Workers Movement (MST) in Brazil, often cited as the largest social movement in the western hemisphere. Using a guarantee in the Brazilian constitution, the MST organizes landless workers to gain occupancy and title of unused lands. The MST has helped more than 250,000 families gain title to over 15 million acres of land. Indeed, it is widely assumed that Brazil was chosen for one of the World Bank's pilot "market-based" land reform projects in order to mute the example it offered to other societies. But South Africa now has its own Landless Peoples' Movement (LPM), and similar efforts exist in India and many countries throughout Latin America.

■

FOR FURTHER INFORMATION:
www.foodfirst.org
www.landaction.org

Citizens Network on Essential Services • Takoma Park, Maryland USA

In February 2002, the World Bank Group's Board of Executive Directors adopted a Private Sector Development (PSD) Strategy, which transforms the operations of the institution by, among other things, calling for an expansion of the role of the private sector in the economies of borrowing countries. Importantly, the strategies define "private sector" to include any non-state organizations, including non-governmental organizations (NGOs), as well as for-profit firms. The institution's strategies for each sector (e.g., education, health, rural development, water, etc.) must be consistent with the PSD Strategy.

The U.S. government promoted the PSD Strategy and now links its financial contributions to the World Bank, specifically IDA, to implementation of the strategy.

The PSD Strategy is widening the gap between rich and poor because it attracts investment capital to poor countries by carving out lucrative markets, and saddles the government with responsibility for unprofitable services. This creates systems of separate and unequal services.

The PSD Strategy liberalizes investment and services in parallel with investment and services talks under the auspices of the World Trade Organization (WTO). If services are subject to the rules of the WTO's General Agreement on Trade in Services (GATS), it could undercut government capacity to protect the public interest.

The PSD Strategy:

- accelerates privatization (especially privatization of basic services – water, health and education) and shrinks the role of government. The World Bank's private-sector-oriented affiliate, the International Finance Corporation (IFC), will team up with the International Development Association (IDA), the World Bank's concessional lending body, to privatize services in low-income countries, including "frontier" areas, such as health and education programs and basic infrastructure.

- liberalizes investment regimes through a new generation of adjustment loans.

- expands direct lending to small and medium-sized enterprises, including via microfinance, while at the same time removing any financial subsidy in the loans.

Many borrowing governments resist the top-heavy distributional and developmental impact of PSD operations. Since there is strong political resistance to the PSD agenda in many countries, the World Bank plans to lend primarily to "reforming" states.

As a consequence of privatization, governments are contracting. In Uganda, out of a total of 22 ministries, 12 have lost about 50% of their functions. Some donors are recommending that, where governments are weak, regulatory functions should be contracted out. In extreme cases, Independent Service Authorities (ISAs), which are accountable directly to donors and creditors, assume the responsibilities of governments for the provision of all services.

Strategies to attract private investment include:

- "unbundling," or segregating profit-making from loss-making assets and services, which may involve selling off, leasing, or contracting out financially viable services (e.g., urban water supply) on a commercial basis – that is, with cost-covering user fees.

- offering political and commercial guarantees to offset risks.

- offering subsidies, especially for extending services to poor and remote populations. In other cases, in order to offset the cost of user fees, targeted subsidies can be paid directly to eligible households.

The PSD Strategy is widening the gap between rich and poor because it attracts investment capital to poor countries by carving out lucrative markets, and saddles the government with responsibility for unprofitable services. This creates systems of separate and unequal services. Although the PSD Strategy supports the provision of free primary education and basic health, targeted subsidies for these or other services generally fail to reach the people who need them. Citizens and representative bodies should determine their government's role in service delivery. Efforts to privatize national assets or their distribution robs citizens of control over their country's destiny; doing so through multilateral institutions is a betrayal of democracy. ■

FOR FURTHER INFORMATION:

www.challengeglobalization.org

FTAA, CAFTA, PPP, IIRSA: Latin America's Alphabet Soup of Neoliberalism

ACERCA / Action for Social and Ecological Justice (ASEJ) • Burlington, Vermont USA

The neo-liberal economic model — privatization of state-owned enterprises, reductions in government expenditures, opening of borders for "free trade," and more — has been imposed on Latin America by multilateral institutions which the U.S. dominates, like the World Bank, the IMF and the Inter-American Development Bank (IDB). Neo-liberalism is also promoted globally through the WTO, and regionally with agreements such as the Free Trade Area of the Americas (FTAA) and the Central American Free Trade Agreement (CAFTA) in the Americas. Complementing these "free trade" agreements in Latin America are packages of massive industrial regional infrastructure projects such as the Plan Puebla Panama (PPP), covering the region from Mexico to Panama, and the Integration of Infrastructure in the Region of South America (IIRSA), spanning from Colombia to Argentina.

These packages of free trade projects proposed for the region are not spreading "freedom," nor "developing" the region as their proponents would have it. Rather, these projects are widening the gap between rich and poor and ruthlessly exploiting workers, indigenous peoples, and women while also destroying the environment. Growing disenchantment with the failures of this "free trade" model in Latin America is widely documented, even by its champions such as the IDB, which begins its diagnosis of the region by stating that 62% of all Latin Americans say that neo-liberalism has worsened their economic situation; 72% say that privatization has not been a good idea; and 70% say that the state should maintain control of education, health care, water and electricity services.

If passed, the FTAA and CAFTA will create the regulatory and legal framework for the acceleration of corporate-led globalization in Latin America by guaranteeing multinational corporations control of the region's abundant cheap labor forces, state-owned services such as heath care and electricity and vast natural resources such as oil, gas, minerals, forest products, genetic material, and commercial agriculture. Combined, the infrastructure megaprojects of the PPP and IIRSA further entice corporate exploitation of the region by providing investors with the infrastructure that they demand. Together the FTAA, CAFTA, PPP and IIRSA are pushing to create a single Latin American free trade zone responding to the wishes of global capital and multinational corporations while failing to respond to the majority of peoples' needs. As a result, people are leaving their communities and immigrating to cities and to the United States in search of economic survival, only to face repression and economic hardship there.

If the FTAA, CAFTA, IIRSA and the PPP are fully implemented, they will:

- Deny countries the right to protect vital local industries, selling off the rights to provide essential services such as health care and education, water, and electricity to transnational corporations.

- Displace thousands of rural and indigenous peoples with massive industrial development projects, including hydroelectric dams, mines, oil drilling, commercial agriculture and logging. Much of the rural work force could be pushed into assembly plant jobs in already-overpopulated urban slums or migrate to the Untied States.

- Deny countries the right to regulate speculative investments, leaving national economies vulnerable to transnational financial corporations.

- Turn over the right to exploit natural resources to foreign and multinational corporate interests.

- Give corporations the right to privatize biodiversity and patent and exploit genetic resources and traditional knowledge found mostly in indigenous communities.

- Deny governments the right to reject genetically modified crops.

- Create and privatize a regional energy market controlled by transnational corporations.

But Latin America is resisting with all its might. The election of President Luiz Ignacio "Lula" de Silva in Brazil and President Lucio Gutiérrez in Ecuador, the mass rejection of politicians tarred by neo-liberalism in Argentina, vigorous protests overturning privatizations in Peru and Bolivia, and a long-term mass campaign against privatization that has emboldened the legislature to rebuff the president in El Salvador add up to make the region the key battleground in determining the future of globalization. ∎

FOR MORE INFORMATION:

www.asej.org

Historically, international trade agreements promoted trade in goods by lowering tariff barriers between countries. This changed dramatically with the conclusion of the 'Uruguay Round' trade negotiations in 1994 which established the World Trade Organization (WTO). A U.S.-led initiative succeeded in putting services, in addition to goods, under WTO jurisdiction. Thus, the General Agreement on Trade in Services (GATS) came into being, along with an alphabet soup of other agreements such as Trade-Related Aspects of Intellectual Property Rights (TRIPS).

Under these new agreements, domestic rules and regulations which might affect trade can be considered "non-tariff trade barriers." Global rules favoring foreign investors and transnational corporations can now trump local democracy.

GATS reaches into every aspect of our lives. Service providers include nurses and doctors, teachers, lawyers, accountants, ministers, reporters, tourist guides, waitresses, and workers in government agencies such as municipal sewer and water departments. Altogether services make up about 70% of the U.S. economy and more than 60% of the global economy.

All domestic laws and regulations "affecting trade in services" come under GATS rules. They even cover foreign direct investments, such as Suez or Bechtel setting up private water companies in South Africa or Bolivia. While there is an exception for public services, the definition is so narrow that almost no government services qualify.

The GATS rules benefit global corporations and investors at the expense of local communities and democratic government authority, and put local service providers at a disadvantage. Such rules also diminish the power of nations and local communities to shape local economic development, promote local culture, provide public services, or advance the rights of women, minority populations and indigenous peoples.

One rule, national treatment, says that foreign corporations must be treated at least as well as domestic companies. Another, most favored nation, says corporations from one WTO member country can't be treated more favorably than those from another country.

Even if there is no discrimination, GATS rules on domestic regulation say that regulations must not be "more burdensome than necessary to ensure the quality of the service." Just how this will be applied is still being negotiated. In addition, under market access rules, governments can't limit the number of service providers or require local participation such as through a joint venture.

Some GATS rules apply to all services, while others (national treatment and market access) apply only to services countries put on their "schedule of commitments." Once commitments are made, countries cannot realistically turn back. Secret trade tribunals are given the authority to determine whether national, state and local laws comply with GATS rules. Non-compliance triggers economic sanctions if the laws are not changed.

The GATS regime reinforces the IMF/World Bank agenda to promote privatization of public services through structural adjustment/poverty reduction requirements and targeted loans. GATS rules tend to lock in privatization and deregulation resulting from these policies.

The GATS commitment to "progressive liberalization" of all services is echoed by the World Bank and IMF, which are committed to liberalization as the most efficient path toward providing the poor with services.

This misguided ideology ignores the fact that for-profit service providers, often powerful transnational corporations, serve only those who can pay. This "cream skimming" results in the exclusion of many people, particularly in developing countries, from essential health, education, and water services.

Now WTO member countries are engaged in secret bilateral negotiations to extend the reach of GATS to more services through a process of requests and offers to be concluded by 2005. Despite claims that GATS would not cover public services, leaked documents confirm that the European Commission has requested that many countries, including the U.S., open up their public water/sewer systems and postal systems to foreign competition.

GATS campaigners are calling for a moratorium on GATS negotiations. All requests and offers must be made public. Essential services should be removed from GATS/WTO jurisdiction. Meanwhile the U.S. is pressing to get complete coverage of services in the FTAA negotiations by eliminating the "schedule of commitments." Activists must be ever vigilant to guard against WTO-mandated corporate takeovers of more and more aspects of our lives. ■

FOR FURTHER INFORMATION:

www.thealliancefordemocracy.org

THE WORLD BANK AND FREE TRADE: WORKING IN HARMONY

Jubilee USA Network / RESULTS • Washington, DC USA

The G7 and other rich countries advocate strongly for national interests through their representatives who sit on the Executive Boards of the IMF and World Bank. Central to the board members' efforts is helping their investors penetrate foreign markets and out-compete those markets' domestic companies. Therefore, they support IMF and World Bank loans to poor countries conditioned on lowering trade barriers and cutting state subsidies to domestic companies. These policies allow foreign investors from rich countries to more easily enter into borrowing countries' domestic markets, while the subsidy cuts weaken the existing domestic companies in the face of increased competition from investors.

The G7 governments justify imposing trade liberalization on countries of the Global South and the former Soviet bloc by holding up neo-liberal economic theory as the proper model for all countries to follow if they wish to achieve economic development. However, all of the wealthy countries, including the East Asian "tiger" economies, industrialized with the assistance of trade protection and subsidy support for domestic companies — NOT as a result of adopting neo-liberal policies.

The result of the last 20 years of trade liberalization in much of the Global South has been "de-industrialization," which has wiped out domestic industries through increased competition from foreign investors and reduced subsidies from the state. Trade policies have undermined the ability of poor countries to diversify their economies away from simple agricultural or natural resource exports, deepening their vulnerability to the fluctuation of world market prices for their goods.

Global investors still fear that poor countries could one day re-regulate their economies, or attempt to reintroduce trade protection or subsidies, so they have introduced legal mechanisms that give global corporate investors the rights to sue governments if they attempt to undo the years of trade liberalization. Such mechanisms are referred to as "investors' rights" and are being encoded among the rules of the World Trade Organization (WTO). These new legal mechanisms will provide foreign investors with the confidence that structural adjustment reforms of the last 20 years will be "locked-in" (to use the actual language of WTO documents).

The trade liberalization policies of the IMF and World Bank loan conditions fit well with the legal rules of WTO membership. The three institutions began increasing the coordination of their overlapping efforts with formal "policy coherence agreements" in the late 1990s. The WTO realized that many of the technical requirements of its rules would be out of reach for many developing countries which lack capacity in their trade and customs ministries.

To facilitate the common goal of further trade liberalization, the World Bank began giving "trade capacity-building" loans specifically designed to enhance countries' capacity for complying with WTO and other trade liberalization rules and requirements. These new loans will both increase countries' entanglement in the global trading system dominated by the Global North and deepen their debt to the World Bank.

The World Bank admits that the global trading system is unfairly stacked in favor of the rich countries, and that the rich countries don't actually play by the free trade rules they force on poorer countries. However, the World Bank's remedy is to call on the rich countries to open their markets to greater access for the poor countries, so that all countries, rich and poor alike, would be moving towards the neo-liberal economic vision of global free trade. There is every reason, however, to suspect that powerful countries would continue to

DEREGULATION

violate the principles of free trade. It would be far better for the global institutions to allow impoverished countries some control over their own destinies by endorsing their right to actively regulate trade.

History shows that all countries that have successfully developed have used trade protection, subsidy support, state-owned industries, public transportation, public health, public education, public utilities, and labor rights. But the neo-liberal economic policies pushed by the Global North would prevent the Global South from benefiting from such policies, while conveniently leaving markets in the Global South open for Global North corporations to exploit. These injustices are currently being locked-in by the new binding rules being negotiated within the WTO, with the connivance of the IMF and World Bank.

■

FOR FURTHER INFORMATION:

www.results.org
www.jubileeusa.org

International Rivers Network • Berkeley, California USA

The World Bank has poured more than $60 billion into large dams. For almost 50 years, such projects seemed a perfect expression of the institution's development paradigm: Massive, centralized investments in physical infrastructure were supposed to spur economic growth, and over time the wealth they generated would trickle down to benefit a society's poor.

Projects such as the Chixoy Dam in Guatemala, Kedung Ombo in Indonesia, Sardar Sarovar in India, Tarbela in Pakistan and Yacyreta on the border between Argentina and Paraguay have demonstrated that in reality, large dams supported by the World Bank resulted in systematic environmental destruction, widespread misery, and financial chaos. In 1993, the Bank was forced to withdraw from the Sardar Sarovar dam after a successful grassroots campaign.

Throughout the 1990s, non-governmental organizations (NGOs) and social movements became more effective in stopping destructive dam projects. In many cases dam opponents were able to demonstrate that less destructive and less expensive alternatives for water and energy development were available. In 1997, the World Commission on Dams (WCD), comprising representatives of governments, NGOs, academia, dam-building corporations, and social movements, was created in order to carry out the first independent, comprehensive evaluation of the impacts of large dams. The World Bank at first embraced the WCD process, hoping that it would bring about a new international consensus on how to build dams.

As it turned out, the WCD report, which was published in November 2000, vindicated much of what the NGOs had been saying for years: "In too many cases," the WCD found, "an unacceptable and often unnecessary price has been paid" to secure the benefits of large dams. According to the report, international financial institutions "played a key strategic role globally in spreading the technology, lending legitimacy to emerging dam projects, training future engineers and government agencies, and leading financing arrangements."

The WCD report put forward seven "strategic priorities" and 26 "policy principles," which included prior informed consent for indigenous peoples, demonstrable public acceptance through negotiated agreements with all other affected communities, comprehensive assessments of needs and options, and addressing the unresolved legacy of existing dams.

Once the WCD report was published, the World Bank changed its position. In public it still claimed to support the Commission's Strategic Priorities, and said it would implement them in a new Water Resources Sector Strategy. Behind the scenes, the World Bank decided to ignore the WCD recommendations, and attacked institutions which were prepared to adopt them.

In February 2003, the World Bank's Executive Board approved a new Water Resources Sector Strategy (WRSS). Contrary to earlier announcements, the new strategy ignores the WCD recommendations completely. Instead, it attempts to promote increased investment in large dams under the euphemism of "high-reward / high-risk hydraulic infrastructure" projects. One month later, a panel consisting of water company executives, representatives of the World Bank and sister institutions, and private lenders managed to call for more aid money for large dams while making no mention of the findings and recommendations of the WCD.

"We think that it is unwise to dismiss without justification or explanation the recommendations of the first-ever global review of dams reached through consensus and developed through an extensive participatory process with support from the World Bank," the members of the WCD had commented on a draft of the WRSS. Yet in the water sector, the World Bank is clearly bent on repeating its earlier mistakes. ∎

FOR FURTHER INFORMATION:

www.dams.org
www.irn.org

THE WORLD BANK'S CORPORATE AGENDA:
ENRON AND OIL FOR THE GLOBAL NORTH

*Sustainable Energy & Economy Network (SEEN) / Institute for Policy Studies •
Washington, DC USA*

The World Bank began to invest in oil and gas production in 1977, following the Organization of Petroleum Exporting Countries (OPEC) oil embargo and oil price shocks of the 1970s. The U.S. – an oil- and gas-dependent country – needed to diversify its sources of non-OPEC oil and gas. Administration officials were concerned that OPEC had a virtual monopoly on the fuels, and could raise prices at whim. Another concern, particularly for Northern investors, was the fact that, as oil prices rose, so too did developing countries' inability to service their debt. The U.S. worried that these countries, already strapped for cash, would default on their loans from U.S. banks.

In a July 1981 report, the Assistant Secretary of the U.S. Treasury prescribed measures the World Bank should take to encourage private investment in oil and gas development. The report noted the World Bank's pivotal role as a multilateral investor that encouraged private investment in projects. The report strongly suggested that the World Bank encourage developing countries privatize their energy resources — "to remove impediments and adopt policies which foster private sector involvement in energy development."

The report reveals that the U.S. Treasury wanted to increase investment in the oil and gas sector in least developed countries (LDCs), primarily in order to "expand and diversify global energy supplies to enhance security of supplies and reduce OPEC market power over oil prices." Treasury also wanted to ensure that developing countries were able to service their debt payments.

The report's authors also reveal their awareness that the U.S. Government was not held in high esteem by many developing countries, and therefore, the World Bank, perceived as a neutral third party, would be more successful in advancing the oil and gas agenda than the U.S.

This agenda — of privatizing state-owned oil and gas companies, as well as power suppliers — remained a high priority at the World Bank. But it was not until the 1990s, when the World Bank began to push both power sector deregulation and oil and gas privatization, that the Bank's agenda began to correspond to that of the fast-growing Enron Corporation.

By 1991, India was the World Bank's largest client. After decades of economic protectionism and heavily subsidized power production, India was under heavy pressure from the lender to change its policies and allow private capital into certain sectors, particularly its petroleum sector. Prime Minister Narasimha Rao decided to bow to World Bank pressure and allowed foreign direct investment into the country. Power sector privatization plans drawn up by the World Bank soon followed.

It was shortly thereafter that Enron came into the picture. Claiming to be one of the "world's leading power companies," Enron proposed to set up a natural gas power plant in the town of Dabhol, in the western Indian state of Maharasthra. At that time, the size of the Dabhol power plant, 2500 megawatts, would more than double Enron's power production globally.

The 1992 memorandum of understanding between Enron, General Electric, and the Maharasthra State Electricity Board stated that the MSEB would owe Enron $35 billion over the life of the contract, regardless of how much power the state consumed. This amounted to the single largest purchase in the history of India.

Meanwhile, Enron began to lobby the World Bank for support of the Dabhol project. Though the World Bank ultimately refused to support it, citing the "adverse financial impact" the arrangement would have on the MSEB, Enron succeeded in gaining financial backers at the U.S.'s Overseas Private Investment Corporation, the U.S. Export-Import Bank, and elsewhere. Enron also succeeded in garnering considerable World Bank Group financing for other projects — $761 million for 12 projects over the last decade.

The World Bank's agenda of privatization and deregulation of energy and power sectors facilitated the entry of unscrupulous corporations, including Enron, into some of the poorest countries in the world, where they have profited handsomely. As in Dabhol, India, the changes they introduced made things worse for the poor: the price of power rose, power was unreliable and less accessible to the poorest, and public debt mounted. Protests and riots — even deaths — ensued. ■

FOR FURTHER INFORMATION:

www.seen.org

Export Credit Agencies: The Dirtiest Secret of Globalization

Pacific Environment • Oakland, California USA

Export Credit Agencies and Investment Insurance Agencies, commonly known as ECAs, are public agencies that provide government-backed loans and insurance to private corporations from their home country to do business abroad, particularly in the financially and politically risky developing world. Most industrialized nations have at least one ECA, which is usually an official or quasi-official branch of their government.

ECAs are collectively the largest sources of public financial support for foreign corporate investment in industrial projects in the developing world. It is estimated that ECA support for oil, gas and mining projects now eclipses that of all multilateral development banks such as the World Bank Group. Half of all new greenhouse gas-emitting industrial projects in developing countries have some form of ECA support.

ECAs also finance large-scale dams, mining projects, road development into pristine tropical forests, oil pipelines, chemical and industrial facilities, and forestry and plantation schemes, to name a few. Many of these projects displace communities and destroy livelihoods, leaving affected people with little or no recourse.

ECAs often back such projects even though the World Bank Group and other multilateral banks find them too risky and potentially harmful to support. Because most of these projects are highly risky due to their environmental, political, social and cultural impacts, most would not come to life without the support and financial backing of ECAs. Hence, ECAs are strategic development linchpins that play an enormous part in the harmful impacts of corporate globalization.

ECAs account for the single biggest component of developing country debt. In recent years they accounted for some 16% of total debt, and 38% of debt owed to official agencies.

ECA financing often pushes countries to create debt to pay back loans for projects that are inconsistent with the goals of sustainable development. Thus, to the extent that excessive or inappropriate developing country debt loads shackle the sustainable development process in these countries, ECAs are in large part responsible.

ECAs are also frequently involved in supporting the export of arms and military equipment to war-torn countries. For example, UK-made Hawk fighter jets and US- made Black Hawk helicopters are exported to Indonesia, Colombia and other countries known for their repressive regimes. These sales are facilitated by ECAs.

Since 1996, NGOs from many countries have joined forces in an international campaign on the ECAs. The goals and demands of the campaign are best described in the Jakarta Declaration for Reform of Official Export Credit and Investment Insurance Agencies, endorsed by over 400 NGOs following a May 2000 international ECA reform strategy session in Jakarta, Indonesia (see www.eca-watch.org/jakarta_engl.html). While focusing on the impacts of ECAs in Indonesia, the Jakarta Declaration has a global "call for reform" that includes:

- Transparency, public access to information, and consultation by ECAs and the (Organization for Economic Cooperation and Development) OECD ECA Working Party;

- Binding common environmental and social guidelines and standards that are no lower or less rigorous than those of the World Bank Group and OECD Development Assistance Committee;

- The adoption of explicit human rights criteria guiding the operations of ECAs;

- The adoption of binding criteria and guidelines to end ECA abetting of corruption;

- The adoption of a commitment only to finance economically productive investments;

- The adoption of comprehensive relief for developing countries for ECA debt.

The current practices of the ECAs embody a form of corrupt, opaque, environmentally and socially destructive globalization compatible with and comparable to those of the World Trade Organization and the World Bank, and IMF. ■

FOR FURTHER INFORMATION:

www.eca-watch.org

In 1983, a bank devoted to providing the poorest of Bangladesh with miniscule loans was established. This unique institution, the Grameen Bank, had the objective of helping the poor survive and in the process creating a sustainable and self-sufficient path out of poverty.

More than a decade later, World Bank president James Wolfensohn, together with then vice president for special programs, Ismail Serageldin and a group of donor agencies formed the Consultative Group to Assist the Poorest (CGAP). CGAP is a consortium of 29 bilateral and multilateral donor agencies which support microfinance. CGAP serves microfinance institutions (MFIs) and donors through the development of technical tools and services, the delivery of training, strategic advice and technical assistance, and research on innovations.

In the first three years of its existence, CGAP played a pivotal role in developing a common language for the sector, and catalyzing the movement towards what it characterized as "best practice performance standards." Unfortunately much of the emphasis within its best practices seemed to ignore, and in some cases even undermine, the valuable role of microfinance as a poverty alleviation tool.

In its first phase, CGAP's Policy Advisory Group agreed to the following definition to guide its work: "The poor live below their nation's poverty line and the poorest are the bottom half of that group." However, few if any of its initiatives were targeted towards increasing outreach of MFIs to "the poorest." By the end of its first phase in June 1998, CGAP seemed to be at the forefront of a group of donors and others that held and promoted the conventional wisdoms -- or myths -- that 1) it was too costly to identify and motivate the poorest, 2) if you did include the poorest, you could not build financially self-sufficient institutions.

These myths have been challenged by facts on the ground as more and more institutions have proven that microfinance can reach the poorest, that it can have a significant impact on their poverty levels, and that it can be delivered by financially self-sufficient institutions. In addition, a comprehensive study on microfinance conducted by World Bank staff and published in 1998, showed that borrowing from a microcredit program is estimated to reduce moderate poverty among participants by as much as 20 percent and extreme poverty by as much as 22 percent.

CGAP was renewed for an additional five years and in its second phase, referred to as CGAP2, appeared to be slowly attempting to move its focus back towards the poorest. One of the CGAP2 strategic themes focused on increasing poverty outreach of MFIs. In addition, in 1999, the organization hired two full-time poverty specialists to identify pro-poor innovations and disseminate "best practice" lessons related to poverty outreach.

However, this positive move seems to have been short-lived. CGAP has now entered its third phase, CGAP3, and its strategy paper emphasizes a shift towards a more diverse range of organizations with different objectives to enable outreach to a broader range of poor clients. This almost certainly means a departure from MFI efforts to reach the poorest. Most telling is the consortium's change of name from the Consultative Group to Assist the Poorest to the Consultative Group to Assist the Poor. Despite its initial enthusiasm, the World Bank estimates that an average of $168 million in funding is approved each year for microfinance -- less than one percent of Bank resources approved annually.

But the Bank's influence, mostly exercised through CGAP, goes beyond the amount it lends. By defining microcredit in particular ways, it can shift the entire sector's priorities. The World Bank's entry into microcredit lending, with its attempt to impose "best practices" and its focus on borrowers with greater access to the conventional credit system, may prove to be the biggest obstacle to this innovative idea for the most impoverished. ■

"East Timor is small, peaceful, and unified. East Timor should be an international success story. Why can't they get it right?" East Timorese people and international friends have repeatedly asked this question as they observe international financial institutions (IFIs), the United Nations, and other aid agencies try to rebuild and develop East Timor after 24 years of brutal Indonesian military occupation.

Asia's poorest country faces many hurdles. According to the 2002 UNDP Human Development Report, over 40% of the population lives on less than 55 cents per day. Virtually all government sectors face extreme hardships, lacking funds and trained personnel, largely due to a legacy of Portuguese colonialism and Indonesian occupation.

The Indonesian military occupation shattered hundreds of thousands of lives through murder, rape, torture and starvation.

IFIs involved in East Timor's reconstruction employed the correct terminology, emphasizing "empowerment," poverty reduction and sustainability. But in East Timor, as elsewhere, words on paper have not always matched reality.

Following East Timor's independence referendum, the military and its militia proxies destroyed more than 75% of East Timor's infrastructure and displaced two-thirds of its population. East Timor finally achieved formal independence on May 20, 2002.

The initial international response to East Timor's destruction was a flood of at-times misdirected international assistance. IFIs involved in East Timor's reconstruction employed the correct terminology, emphasizing "empowerment," poverty reduction and sustainability. But in East Timor, as elsewhere, words on paper have not always matched reality. IFIs continue to push the same misguided policies in East Timor as they have elsewhere. NGOs and the East Timorese government have resisted — with occasional success.

IFI involvement in a post-conflict East Timor started early. Just weeks after international peacekeepers arrived in 1999, the World Bank led a three-week Joint Assessment Mission. Participants included East Timorese leaders, the IMF, Asian Development Bank (ADB), UN, and representatives of other major donors. The IFIs quickly gained control of significant portions of donor funds. By December, donors had established a Trust Fund for East Timor (TFET) with the World Bank as its trustee. The ADB and the World Bank manage TFET projects, which have included infrastructure, water, power, microfinance, health, education, private sector development, agriculture, economic capacity building, and community development. By mid-November 2002, almost $174 million had been committed to various TFET projects. Throughout the duration, the IMF has provided technical assistance and policy guidance to impose its view of a "sound" macroeconomic framework.

In early 2002, the World Bank gained administrative control over budget support funds to cover the government's post-independence financing gap, estimated at $90 million over three years. The Finance Minister at the time vigorously opposed World Bank trust fund management, concerned with the World Bank's record in other poor countries. She soon resigned and was replaced by a Finance Minister more amenable to the IFIs. The East Timorese government continues to fight IFI conditionality on the trust fund. Not wanting to mortgage the future by incurring debt, it has also managed to maintain a "no loans" policy.

The World Bank has pressed for privatization of the power and communications sectors, while the ADB advocates water privatization. Following IMF advice, the UN administration and subsequent East Timorese government adopted the U.S. dollar as the official currency. The IMF has advanced free market liberalization, discouraging government price controls and labor protections. The U.S. Agency for International Development (USAID) is promoting a user fee model for healthcare in East Timor and private sector development through export crop production, particularly coffee — despite the plunge in coffee prices that has already pushed countries like Nicaragua and Ethiopia into desperate circumstances.

IFIs and the UN often cite East Timor as a pilot project from which other post-conflict countries can learn. However, it seems that IFIs have not yet learned the lessons taught by the painful experiences of so many others in the Global South. ■

FOR FURTHER INFORMATION:

www.etan.org

Movement for National Land and Agricultural Reform (MONLAR) •
Ethulkotte SRI LANKA

In recent years, the World Bank and IMF have increased their involvement in "post-conflict" countries at the very beginning of their recovery process. As a country celebrates peace, the World Bank and its partners offer to help in designing a viable post-war economy. Naturally, that economy will be driven by the neo-liberal policies that the World Bank spends so much energy encouraging other countries to accept. In post-conflict societies, which come closer to "starting from scratch," the World Bank has the greatest opportunity and leverage to make its will prevail.

In Sri Lanka, which has suffered one of the world's longest and most brutal civil wars, the vigilance of an active and informed civil society has not been subverted by the eagerness to be done with war. On October 24, 2002 over 15,000 Sri Lankan citizens took to the streets — just one of the many expressions of the broad grassroots movement poised against the newly proposed economic policy package agreed upon by the World Bank, the IMF, and the Sri Lankan Government. These policies are based on the World Bank's poverty reduction strategy paper (PRSP), "Connect to Growth: Sri Lanka's Poverty Reduction Strategy."

The PRSP was introduced by the IMF and World Bank in 1999 as the new way of constructing economic reform programs in partnership with national civil societies. In many countries there are disputes about how "participatory" the process has been; in Sri Lanka, the civil society groups the World Bank claims to have consulted had no idea they were participating in a "poverty reduction strategy" process.

Immediately after the paper's appearance, 36 separate pieces of legislation were sent by the government to Parliament for urgent consideration. The bills corresponded directly to reforms the PRSP said were necessary, and it soon became clear that their passage was a pre-requisite for securing any funding from the international financial institutions.

The proposed legislation would expedite the process of privatizing the state banks, the highly-profitable state insurance corporation, the electricity board, post office, revenue department, the workers' pension fund, water resources, sanitary services, health, much of education, railways, phosphate mines, fish hatcheries, forests, and more. Rather than reduce poverty, this will simply perpetuate the already blatant wealth discrepancy by denying many crucial services to those who are unable to pay for them, and by directing profits into private hands rather than the public treasury.

The land reform bills are particularly far-reaching, aiming to relocate 1.8 million families who live on small subsistence farms to urban areas. This would allow corporate investors to implement large-scale commercial farming with chemical inputs. This relies on the assumption that there will be ample non-farm employment opportunities to absorb the millions of displaced and unemployed individuals created by this reform. Unfortunately, this assumption is contradicted by Sri Lanka's past experiences. The export garment sector, the only industry to grow in the past 25 years, has been experiencing a rapid decline in production due to the scheduled termination of the U.S. and European Union garment import quotas in 2005. The proposed labor law reforms would guarantee that those who do obtain employment will most likely be overworked, underpaid, and subjected to poor working conditions.

Critics charge that the proposed policies are an expansion of the economic strategy that has failed Sri Lanka for the last 24 years. An unprecedented alliance of labor unions, farmers' groups, faith-based organizations, and others has formed to oppose the PRSP and associated legislation. At this writing (May 2003), they have succeeded in stalling two-thirds of the bills in Parliament, and have made the program a subject of national debate. ■

FOR FURTHER INFORMATION:
www.geocities.com/monlarslk/

Until the end of the 1990s, Argentina was the model country IMF economists pointed to in promoting the free market economic model. Now, it is struggling to overcome a prolonged and deep economic crisis that has been compared to the Great Depression of the 1930s.

With the strong backing of the IMF and World Bank in the early 1990s, Argentina began to de-regulate trade and financial markets and privatize virtually every public service (including the postal service). The government tied its own hands further by pegging the value of its currency to the U.S. dollar. Initially the currency peg attracted foreign investment, since it seemed like the greatest protection against currency fluctuations.

But when the value of the U.S. dollar began to rise in the mid-1990s, things in Argentina began to fall apart. Argentine exports lost competitiveness and industry began to decline, causing a jump in unemployment. Simultaneously, social security privatization under World Bank sponsorship led to a decline in government revenues, since contributions to social security were diverted to private pension funds. As revenues fell, the government turned to the IMF for help in meeting loan payments. In return, the IMF demanded deep cuts in public spending that further cut domestic demand and stoked social unrest.

Although Argentina's grossly overvalued currency was a major factor in the collapse, other free market reforms exacerbated the problems. Once trade barriers and capital controls had been lifted, the government was powerless to address the looming trade deficit and the flight of capital. Privatization led to reduced access to services for the poor and middle class. Millions lost health coverage as private international insurers pressured providers to cut costs. Argentine banks were sold to foreign firms, which cut back lending to small and medium enterprises. Stripped of protections, private employers were pressured to become "lean and mean" through mass layoffs. Along with the IMF and World Bank, they also lobbied for labor law reform that further weakened unions. All this fueled the anger that exploded in deadly riots in December 2001 and brought about the country's financial crash. Unable to meet debt service payments to foreign banks, Argentina declared the largest default in world history that same month.

The IMF never admitted any wrong-doing in Argentina. Instead it blamed the country's collapse on excessive public spending and the currency peg (which they initially supported and helped sustain, but now claim was a purely homegrown policy). Even as the economy was in a free fall throughout 2002 (GDP declined 12 percent), the IMF continued to demand increased austerity and other structural reforms as conditions for restarting lending to the credit-strapped country. A rising tide of public opinion against further concessions to the IMF pressured the government to tell the IMF that if it didn't agree to defer loan payments, Argentina would default on its IMF obligations, just as it had to private bankers. In January 2003, the IMF board, led by the G-7 country governments, recognized that the IMF's credibility was in jeopardy throughout Latin America, and forced IMF management to concede to a "rollover" of Argentina's loans.

The Argentine experience is a lesson of the extreme dangers of the radical free market system, but it is also a lesson in the power of resistance. While the people of Argentina continue to suffer, their unified opposition against the IMF and World Bank has had a substantial and positive impact. ■

FOR FURTHER INFORMATION:

www.ips-dc.org

HUMAN RIGHTS, OIL, & INDIGENOUS COMMUNITIES: THE WORLD BANK IN THE ANDEAN REGION

Center for Economic and Social Rights • Quito ECUADOR

In Ecuador, one can hardly discuss the World Bank without talking of oil. The World Bank's fixation on oil as an indispensable export has put it on a collision course with indigenous people who inhabit the richest oil fields and whose rights are under constant threat by the oil industry. The World Bank's latest initiative for overcoming this collision is to redefine the rights violations associated with oil activities as socio-economic or socio-environmental conflicts. Rather than having to promote basic rights at the risk of impeding oil development, the World Bank's task then becomes "conflict resolution."

In the Andean countries of Venezuela, Ecuador, Colombia, Peru and Bolivia, the World Bank has historically been the determining factor in the development of the oil industry. But the focus on oil has led to skewed and unstable economies and political systems. From the mid-1970s through 2000, roughly corresponding to the period of oil expansion, the region's foreign debt grew from about $12 billion to $178 billion. In that same period, overall poverty and unemployment also increased. Oil riches have rarely trickled beyond a select few.

From 1970 to 1994, oil production in Latin America grew approximately 50%. Currently, oil is the primary export in Venezuela, Colombia, Peru and Ecuador.

Since the early 1990's, World Bank loans in the region have been guided by two overriding goals. The first is privatization. Through new laws and institutions pushed by the World Bank, the role of the state in the oil business was reduced. The second was legislation and policies on environment and indigenous peoples. This latter emphasis resulted from large-scale opposition to the World Bank's secretive, anti-environmental and anti-indigenous policies.

With its re-fashioning of human rights violations as "conflicts" between equally legitimate parties, and its self-designation as a facilitator of "conflict resolution," the World Bank has effectively foreclosed the right of communities to simply reject outside exploitation of their land and resources. The World Bank has essentially decided that indigenous rights would have to be weighed against the economic interest of other "stakeholders."

The World Bank is determined to "resolve the conflicts" without impeding oil activities. That requires the World Bank to neutralize any activity that threatens oil extraction, even if that activity is the defense of human rights. In the process, essential rights for indigenous communities, rights backed by constitutions and international law, including territorial rights, the right to informed participation, the

'...SO YOU SEE, THE ENTIRE FUTURE OF THE INTERNATIONAL FINANCIAL SYSTEM HINGES ON YOUR CAPACITY FOR QUICK RECOVERY AND VAST ECONOMIC GROWTH.'

right to influence and benefit from development processes, the right to live in a healthy environment, and the right to maintain and enjoy one's culture, may be compromised or even ignored. Indeed, the very acknowledgment of the inherent rights of local communities threatens to trump the status of "stakeholder" corporations, and so is obscured by the World Bank.

Despite numerous "dialogues" sponsored by the World Bank and new consultation and participation regulations in the Andean countries, the indigenous groups have not been won over. The World Bank's initial Indigenous People's Policy (IPP) was widely acknowledged to be unacceptable, and the revised version has likewise been widely criticized.

Meanwhile, the legitimizing cover of "dialogue," "consultation," and "conflict resolution" continues to undermine efforts by indigenous communities to oppose destructive oil development. The facilitators from the World Bank continue to be unwilling to hear a simple "no." In "conflict resolution," the deck is stacked against the weaker players. Keeping in mind that a year's income for ExxonMobil is three times the national budget of Ecuador, and an oil company can buy off communities with hardly a blip on their expense sheets, what is the future of indigenous people confronting Big Oil?

The World Bank may argue that, in theory, oil should make everyone better off by creating vast wealth. But after 30 years of experience, and numerous World Bank financed studies, the evidence that the dependence on oil has caused more harm than good is impossible to hide. Given the World Bank's explicit mission to help the poor, how can it justify consistently putting the interests of multinational corporations before those of local communities? Those affected by oil would be justified in asking if the World Bank's mission, like the rights of these communities, has been compromised by the ever-present U.S. need to diversify its sources of oil. ■

EarthRights International provided translation and editorial assistance for this article.

FOR FURTHER INFORMATION:

www.cesr.org

Behind a banner reading, "End Exploitation of Domestic Workers in the World Bank/IMF Family," housekeepers, nannies, cooks, and other workers who have been abused by their World Bank and IMF employers have been mobilizing to create change.

These domestic workers – virtually all women from impoverished countries in Asia, Africa, and Latin America – are part of a special visa program known as G-5, under which officials with the World Bank, the IMF and other international agencies are allowed to bring live-in household help from overseas. Each year, over 1,000 domestic workers enter the U.S. on G-5 visas to work for employees of the World Bank and IMF. For some, it is a satisfactory job. But others, who believe they are coming to fulfill their American dream, find themselves living out a nightmarish reality.

Each year, over 1,000 domestic workers enter the U.S. to work for employees of the World Bank and the IMF. For some, it is a satisfactory job; others find themselves living out a nightmarish reality.

Although these domestic workers are entitled to the full protection of U.S. labor laws, exploitation and abuse at the hands of World Bank/IMF employees are rampant. It is not uncommon to hear reports of women being paid 50 cents or a dollar an hour and, in other cases, forced to work for months or years with no pay at all. Many women find themselves working nearly around the clock, seven days a week. The World Bank/IMF official also typically tells the worker that she should not talk to anyone, leave the house unaccompanied or use the telephone. At times, psychological, sexual, and/or physical abuse occurs and women are held in involuntary servitude, living as virtual prisoners in the homes they clean. While the State Department and international institutions are well aware of these abuses, they have failed for decades to establish systems of protection or oversight.

World Bank and IMF officials are granted a "special privilege" to legally bring hired help to the U.S. Unfortunately, once the paperwork has been filed, the institutions take a "hands-off" approach. As a result, modern-day slavery is been practiced in our own backyard. The abuse symbolizes what is wrong with the way these institutions operate. If they can't make sure that their employers aren't violating human and labor rights and subjecting people to poverty, how are they suppose to make educated claims about "helping" people worldwide?

Many of the women originally come to the United States because the structural adjustment programs imposed by the IMF and World Bank in their home country have sapped their economic opportunities. However, once they arrive, they find themselves in double jeopardy as their economic options are again stifled by the same people and similar institutional indifference.

The Break the Chain Campaign has sent World Bank President James Wolfensohn a letter detailing this problem and asking for his personal intervention. For the past four years, the Campaign has been involved in discussions with the World Bank and the IMF but, despite some modest reforms, serious cases of abuse continue. Now the domestic workers themselves are beginning to organize. ■

To get involved, please call +1-202-234-9382 x244, or visit www.ips-dc.org/campaign/index2.htm

ACT LOCALLY FOR GLOBAL JUSTICE: JOIN THE WORLD BANK BONDS BOYCOTT

Center for Economic Justice / World Bank Bonds Boycott • Washington, DC USA

The World Bank (specifically, the IBRD and the IFC) raises roughly $20 billion on the bond market every year. Investors, including churches, city and state government pension funds, universities, mutual fund investors, and union pension funds, are among the potential and actual buyers of World Bank bonds. Through the World Bank Bonds Boycott, people of faith, taxpayers, working people, and students are building political pressure to end harmful World Bank policies, by getting their institutions and cities to commit not to buy World Bank bonds.

The World Bank Bonds Boycott was launched in April 2000 by representatives of economic and environmental justice groups from over 35 countries in the Global South and the United States. The campaign is directed by an International Coordinating Committee with representatives from 14 countries.

Already, more than 80 institutions and municipalities have adopted policies against investing in World Bank bonds. City councils in seven U.S. cities including Milwaukee, San Francisco, Boulder, and Oakland have also adopted resolutions against investment in World Bank bonds. More than two dozen unions, including the 1.5-million-member International Brotherhood of the Teamsters and the 1.4-million-member Service Employees International Union, the

Communications Workers of America, and the American Federation of Government Employees have adopted the World Bank Bonds Boycott. Several dozen religious communities have joined the campaign. Activists working with local Boycott coalitions around the country achieved many of these victories.

The World Bank Bonds Boycott has three demands of the World Bank: 100% debt cancellation for impoverished countries; an end to "structural adjustment" and related policies of privatization and austerity; and an end to lending for environmentally and socially harmful sectors, such as oil, gas, mining and dams.

The strategy of the Boycott is modeled on the successful anti-apartheid divestment movement of the 1980s. Recognizing that the World Bank is vulnerable to challenges to its public image and financing, the Boycott builds strong moral, political, and financial pressure on the World Bank for change. It is not even necessary for institutions to own World Bank bonds to join the Boycott, as the campaign only seeks a policy against future purchase of the bonds, not divestment.

Meanwhile, the campaign is also targeting larger and more financially significant World Bank bond investors such as state employee pension funds, teacher retirement funds, and others. Combined with moral pressure, the financial pressure that the Boycott is generating is becoming a powerful force for fundamental change at the institution.

We know the World Bank is paying attention to the Boycott. In August 2001, the World Bank had high-level staff lobby members of the Boulder city council against the passage of a resolution that would get the city to commit not to invest in World Bank bonds in the future. This generated a rich debate in Boulder and compelled the World Bank to defend its policies in a very public city council debate that was widely reported in the press. The World Bank has also sought (unsuccessfully) to dissuade other investors from joining the Boycott, which indicates their growing concern, and the campaign's growing effectiveness.

Get involved! You can work with your city council, union, church, school, or other institution to pass a resolution against World Bank bonds investment. In fact, there may already be a World Bank Bonds Boycott group working in your town." ∎

FOR FURTHER INFORMATION:
www.worldbankboycott.org

LIST OF ABBREVIATIONS

ADB	Asian Development Bank
ANC	African National Congress
CAFTA	Central American Free Trade Agreement
CGAP	Consultative Group to Assist the Poorest
ECA	Export Credit Agency
EPZ	Export Processing Zone
EU	European Union
FTAA	Free Trade Area of the Americas
FTAP	Fair and Transparent Arbitration Mechanism
G-7/G-8	Group of Seven/ Group of Eight
GATS	General Agreement on Trade in Services
GDP	Gross Domestic Product
GEF	Global Environment Facility
HIPC	Highly Indebted Poor Countries
HIV/AIDS	Human Immunodeficiency Virus/Acquired Immune Deficiency Syndrome
IBRD	International Bank for Reconstruction and Development
ICSID	International Center for Settlement of Investment Disputes
IDA	International Development Association
IDB	InterAmerican Development Bank
IFC	International Finance Corporation
IFI	International Financial Institutions
IIRSA	Integration of Infrastructure in the Region of South America
ILO	International Labor Organization
IMF	International Monetary Fund
IPP	Indigenous People's Policy
ISA	Independent Service Authority
LDC	Less/Least Developed Country
MFI	Microfinance Institution
MIGA	Multilateral Investment Guarantee Agency
MIMIC	Massively Indebted Middle Income Country
MST	Landless Workers Movement (Brazil)
NGO	Non-governmental Organization
OPEC	Organization of Petroleum Exporting Countries
OECD	Organization for Economic Cooperation and Development
PPP	Plan Puebla Panama
PRGF	Poverty Reduction and Growth Facility
PRSP	Poverty Reduction Strategy Paper
PSD	Private Sector Development
SAP	Structural Adjustment Programs
SAPRIN	Structural Adjustment Participatory Review Network
SDRM	Sovereign Debt Restructuring Mechanism
STD	Sexually Transmitted Disease
SUNFED	Special UN Fund for Economic Development
TRIPS	Trade-Related Aspects of Intellectual Property Rights
UN	United Nations
UNDP	United Nations Development Program
UNICEF	United Nations Children's Fund
USAID	United States Agency for International Development
WCD	World Commission on Dams
WRSS	Water Resources Sector Strategy
WTO	World Trade Organization

Suggested sampling of additional resources on the IMF, the World Bank, the WTO, and the Global Economy, and the analysis and movements resisting, challenging, and creating alternative visions for justice and sustainability.

BOOKS

Anderson, Sarah, ed. *Views from the South*. Food First Books, 2000.

Anderson, Sarah, John Cavanagh and Thea Lee. *Field Guide to the Global Economy*. New Press, 2000.

Barlow, Maude and Tony Clarke. *Global Showdown: How the New Activists Are Fighting Global Corporate Rule*. Stoddart Publishing, 2002.

Bello, Walden. *De-Globalization: Ideas for a New World Economy*. Zed Books, 2003.

Bello, Walden, Cunningham, Shea and Rau, Bill. *Dark Victory: The United States and Global Poverty*. Pluto Press, 1999.

Bond, Patrick. *Against Global Apartheid: South Africa Meets the World Bank, IMF and International Finance*. University of Cape Town, 2001.

Broad, Robin, ed. *Global Backlash: Citizen Initiatives for a Just World Economy*. Rowman and Littlefield, 2002.

Caufield, Catherine. *Masters of Illusion: The World Bank and the Poverty of Nations*. Henry Holt and Company, 1997.

Cavanagh, John, and Jerry Mander, eds. *Alternatives to Economic Globalization: A Better World is Possible*. Berrett-Koehler, 2002.

Chang, Ha-Joon. *Kicking Away the Ladder: Development Strategy in Historical Perspective*. Anthem Press, 2002.

Chomsky, Noam. *Profits Over People: Neo-liberalism and Global Order*. Seven Stories Press, 1998.

Collins, Chuck and Felice Yeskel. *Economic Apartheid in America*. New Press, 2000.

Daly, Herman. *Beyond Growth: The Economics of Sustainable Development*. Beacon Press, 1997.

Danaher, Kevin, ed. *50 Years Is Enough: The Case Against the World Bank and the International Monetary Fund*. South End Press, 1994.

Danaher, Kevin, ed. *Democratizing the Global Economy: The Battle Against the World Bank and the IMF*. Common Courage Press, 2001.

Danaher, Kevin. *10 Reasons to Abolish the IMF and World Bank*. Seven Stories Press, 2001.

Fisher, William F. and Antonio Negri, eds. *Another World Is Possible: Popular Alternatives to Globalization at the World Social Forum*. Zed Books, 2003.

Garson, Barbara. *Money Makes The World Go Around*. Penguin, 2002.

George, Susan. *A Fate Worse than Debt: The World Financial Crisis and the Poor*. Grove Press, 1990.

George, Susan. *The Debt Boomerang: How Third World Debt Harms Us All.* Pluto Press, 1991.

George, Susan and Fabrizio Sabelli. *Faith and Credit: The World Bank's Secular Empire.* Westview Press, 1994.

Goldsmith, Edward, and Jerry Mander, eds . *The Case Against the Global Economy and for a Turn Towards Localization.* Sierra Club Books, 1997.

Greider, William. *One World Ready or Not: The Manic Logic of Global Capital.* Simon and Schuster, 1997.

Hertz, Noreena. *The Silent Takeover: Global Capitalism and the Death of Democracy.* Harper Business, 2003.

Klein, Naomi. *Fences and Windows: Dispatches from the Front Lines of the Globalization Debate.* Picador, 2002.

Makhijani, Arjun. *From Global Capitalism to Economic Justice.* Apex Press, 1992.

Payer, Cheryl. *Lent and Lost: Foreign Credit and Third World Development.* Zed Books, 1991.

Rich, Bruce. *Mortgaging the Earth: The World Bank, Environmental Impoverishment, and the Crisis of Development.* Beacon Press Books, 1994.

Shiva, Vandana. *Water Wars, Privatization, Pollution, and Profit.* South End Press, 1997.

Sparr, Pamela, ed. *Mortgaging Women's Lives: Feminist Critique of Structural Adjustment.* Zed Books, 1994.

Stiglitz, Joseph. *Globalization and its Discontents.* W.W. Norton and Company, 2002.

Waring, Marilyn. *If Women Counted.* Harper Collins, 1990.

MAGAZINES/NEWSLETTERS

Economic Justice News
World Bank and IMF updates, campaign news, and action alerts
www.50years.org

Multinational Monitor
Monitors corporate activity in the Global South
www.multinationalmonitor.org

The Nation
Progressive analysis of U.S. political and popular current events
www.thenation.org

The New Internationalist
Progressive analysis of international current events
www.newint.org

WEB SITES

50 Years Is Enough Network..www.50years.org
Action for Social and Economic Justice/ACERCA............www.asej.org
AFL-CIO...www.aflcio.org
Africa Action..www.africaaction.org
Anti-Privitisation Forum ....www.apf.org.za
Bank Information Center ....www.bicusa.org
Bretton Woods Project..www.brettonwoodsproject.org
Center for International Environmental Law ....www.ciel.org
Citizens Network on Essential Services ....www.challengeglobalization.org
EcoNews Africa...www.econewsafrica.org
Essential Action..www.essentialaction.org
Focus on the Global South..www.focusweb.net
Food First..www.foodfirst.org
Foreign Policy In Focus...www.fpif.org
Friends of the Earth International ....www.foei.org
Friends of the Earth, U.S. ....www.foe.org/camps/intl/index.html
Global Exchange ....www.globalexchange.org
Halifax Initiative..www.halifaxinitiative.org
International Confederation of Free Trade Unions ....www.icftu.org
Institute for Policy Studies..www.ips-dc.org
International Rivers Network ....www.irn.org
Jobs with Justice ....www.jwj.org
Jubilee Research...www.jubileeresearch.org
Jubilee USA Network...www.jubileeusa.org
Maryknoll Office for Global Concerns ....www.maryknoll.org
MONLAR...www.geocities.com/monlarslk/
Religious Working Group on the IMF & World Bank......www.sndden.org/rwg/
Results...www.results.org
SAPRIN...www.saprin.org
Social Justice Committee...www.socialjusticecommittee.org
Sustainable Energy & Economy Network.........................www.seen.org
Tanzania Gender Networking Programme ....www.tgnp.co.tz
Third World Network..www.twnside.org.sg
Whirled Bank ....www.whirledbank.org
Women's Environment & Development Organization.........www.wedo.org
World Bank Bonds Boycott ....www.worldbankboycott.org
World Bunk ....www.worldbunk.org
World Development Movement ....www.wdm.org.uk
World Social Forum...www.worldsocialforum.org

MULTILATERAL INSTITUTIONS

International Monetary Fund...www.imf.org
United Nations Conference on Trade and Development..www.unctad.org
United Nations Development Fund for Women.............www.unifem.org
United Nations Development Program.............................www.undp.org
World Bank Group..www.worldbank.org
World Trade Organization...www.wto.org

FILMS AND VIDEOS

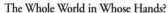

Two Trevors Go To Washington
http://go.to/two.trevors
April 16, 2000 IMF/World Bank protests from the inside and the outside

The Whole World in Whose Hands?
The United Methodist Women's Division - (800) 305-9857
A women's and faith-based approach to the WTO and globalization

To Be A Woman
Visafric Productions - Inter-Church Coalition on Africa (416) 927-1124
Women surviving structural adjustment in Ghana, Zambia, and Uganda

Another World is Possible: Northern Voices at the 2002 World Social Forum
50 Years Is Enough Network – (202) 463-2265
The experiences of U.S. community-based and grassroots groups at the 2002
World Social Forum in Porto Alegre, Brazil

Deadly Embrace: Nicaragua, the World Bank and IMF
http://store.globalexchange.org/deadlyembrace.html
Chronicles Nicaragua's experience of IMF/World Bank policies

SOA: Guns and Greed
www.maryknoll.org or (800)227-8523.
Connections between corporate globalization in Latin America and U.S.
military training at the School of the Americas

Profits of Doom
Available from the BBC - bbcstudies@bbc.co.uk
The struggles against structural adjustment and water privatization in Ghana

Life and Debt
www.lifeanddebt.org
The devastating human costs of structural adjustment and debt in Jamaica

Bill Moyers Report: Trading Democracy
www.cwa-union.org/international/FTAA
Shows how WTO and NAFTA rules favor corporate profits over democracy
and human needs

From the Mountains to the Maquiladoras
www.tirn.org
Laid-off Tennessee factory workers visit Mexican communities where
factories moved

Global Village, Global Pillage
Center for Economic Justice - 202-393-6665.
Overview of the structures of globalization and movements in resistance

T-Shirt Travels
Filmmakers Library 800-555-9815, infor@filmmakers.com
Where do your old clothes go when you donate them?

Profit and Nothing But
First Run Icarus Films - http://www.frif.com/new2001/but.html
Documents the failure of neo-liberal development in Haiti

The Money Lenders: Update 2000
www.richtervideos.com
Critics and defenders debate the IMF and World Bank's impact in Bolivia,
Ghana, Brazil, Thailand and the Philippines

Banking on Life and Debt
Maryknoll World Productions - www.maryknoll.org
Examines the effects of the international financial institutions on Ghana,
Brazil and the Philippines

Its My Life
First Run Icarus Films - http://www.frif.com/new2002/mlife.html
Story of South African AIDS activist Zackie Ashmat, who has HIV but
refuses anti-retrovirals

The War Of Water
Oswaldo Rioja
marcelaolivera@mindspring.com
The people's rebellion against water privatization in Cochabamba, Bolivia